SUTTON SCOTNEY

LIFE AT A COUNTRY STATION

Kevin Robertson

©Kestrel Railway Books and Kevin Robertson 2006

Kestrel Railway Books
PO Box 269
SOUTHAMPTON
SO30 4XR

www.kestrelrailwaybooks.co.uk

All rights reserved.

No part of this publication may be
reproduced, stored in a retrieval system,
transmitted in any form or by any means,
electronic, mechanical, or photocopied,
recorded or otherwise, without the
consent of the publisher in writing.

Printed by the Cromwell Press

ISBN 1905505000

Front cover: The country station. Sutton Scotney from the Wonston road bridge, looking towards Whitchurch, in what were the halcyon days for the railway.

(Tom Palmer courtesy Reg Harvey)

Contents

Preface

This is the third book in the series *Great Western Aspects*. Why choose Sutton Scotney? Well simply because there was a story to be told, and the information was to hand. It is a story that has been a delight to research and compile, and which I hope will enable some more information on what I will confess has always been my personal favourite bit of railway, to be revealed.

With any research (and that involving the Didcot, Newbury, and Southampton spans almost all my adult life) new material gradually comes to hand. A few snippets of information, a photograph or document, many too special to be restricted to the eyes of one person alone. Hence this latest booklet. Not a history, more an appreciation, and as accurate as I can make it, with everything based on fact.

None though would have been possible without the generous help over the years of one the main players, Ernie Penny. Ernie, along with Fred Capon, Ken Alexander, Arthur Watts and several others named in the book, I had the privilege of meeting and all without exception were only too glad to recount their stories. Others I have had to glean information from second-hand – how I would have enjoyed meeting Bob Sullivan!

It is with thanks then to all those named that I submit this work. Thanks also to the family of Ernie for their support and encouragement, their father like the others mentioned needs to be remembered.

I have also of necessity at times drawn on information from my previous works on the DNS line, published by Kestrel Railway Books and Wild Swan. If you are new to *Great Western Aspects,* you might find the two earlier books in the series of interest; these are listed on the last page.

"Times may well change and we change with them" is my final quote in this work, but I for one still sometimes wish to live in the past.

Kevin Robertson, 2006.

Sutton Scotney looking south, depicted in a scene from a contemporary postcard dating from April 1906. This is the earliest view of the station located so far, and it probably appears very much as when first opened 21 years before. The scene would also have been very similar to that recalled by Ernie Penny and Mr Parsons years later, although by that time a number of trees had grown up on the down (east) side of the line behind what was the original signalbox. The small wooden building on the left was a ground frame hut used for controlling the crossover points exiting from goods yard and which are seen in the foreground. Both the trailing connecting and ground frame were removed around 1922 – probably because they needed to be replaced due to wear and with further expense not justified as traffic levels simply did not warrant it. The structure of the ground frame then found a new use as a parcels hut at the far end of the station building. The trailing crossover from the yard was eventually reinstated again after 1943.

Chapter 1

MONDAY 29th SEPTEMBER 1947

Mondays have never been the most popular day of the week. To the working masses the weekend is now but history, and the next a long five, or even five-and-a-half days work away. To the housewife Monday was also traditionally washing day, a day of boiling coppers, steaming kitchens and sculleries, certainly red hands and an aching back by the end of the day. And to the school children, the start of another week, lessons in the three Rs, perhaps, allied to the austere atmosphere of neat rows of desks, hard wooden chairs and a classroom seemingly never free of chalk dust.

Locally at Sutton Scotney, the new week would for most also be likewise similar to the previous. The postman and tradesmen – the milkman, baker, and butcher making their rounds as before whilst on the main roads through the village an amount of traffic would pass, assuming of course that drivers could obtain fuel. Rationing still very real at that time.

These were the days then of austerity, the continuing monotony little altered from day to day and with perhaps little promise of immediate change in the lives of most of the inhabitants of the village.

But for one person at least, Monday 29th September was different. For local man, Ernie Penny, this was the day he "took on" as signalman at the village railway station. (His full name was Ernest, but usually this was shorted to Ernie, or even Ern.)

The term "took on" was used to impart when a new man was considered competent to take over a task. It was regularly used by the traffic department staff in a variety of grades.

Ernie had joined the Great Western Railway in 1946, in what were to be its final years as a private company, nationalisation due to occur on 1st January 1948. The organisation that he joined though was steeped in tradition and that included the Traffic as well as the Signalling and Telegraph Departments. A later example of this being that, although as part of his subsequent signal-box training he was expected to complete the entries in the Train Register, he was not allowed to sign his name

in the book – this was the only permitted by the duty signalman alone.

Ernie had actually started on the railway as a porter at Sutton Scotney, a quiet country station located on the southern half of the erstwhile Didcot, Newbury and Southampton route, some eight miles north of Winchester. Accordingly in applying for the post he was interviewed by the Sutton Scotney Station Master, Mr Parsons. Great emphasis was placed by Mr Parsons on the responsibilities embodied in the position he was applying for, and although there is no record of this interview surviving, it is likely that the importance of the work on the railway would have been outlined in no uncertain terms. Such an approach though was hardly likely to put off Ernie, having lived within earshot of the railway all his life as well as taking a passing interest in its working, he was well aware of what the job entailed.

With a vacancy also at the station for the grade of porter-signalman, sometimes also referred to as signal-porter, and having also quickly proven himself reliable and hard working, Ernie was eventually despatched to Newbury for a visit to Mr Sullivan, the District Inspector responsible for signalling in an area that included Sutton Scotney. Here he would have received another grilling, although this time from a perhaps shrewder man, who was adept at recognising whether an interviewee was a worthwhile candidate to consider.

In Ernie he would have had no doubt, and as there was a permanent vacancy in the signalbox at what was a Grade 5 post at his home station, it was agreed he could learn on the job. Accordingly he was issued with a copy of the red *Signalman's General Instructions,* which supplemented his existing copy of the *GWR Rule Book*. Ernie may well have thought that on his return to Sutton Scotney he would report for signalbox training immediately, but sometimes others can have an alternative view.

Indeed, Mr Parsons did have other ideas, his priorities more in the community his station served – and even more so it seemed in cultivating the display of plants for the station garden. Accordingly he would spend long

Sutton Scotney signalbox and Ernie Penny's new working environment from September 1947 onwards. Located on the east side of the line, next door is the permanent-way hut, both structures dated from 1942/3, the time that the line was upgraded.

(Ernie Penny)

periods each day away, ostensibly on railway business, but it was strange how often he returned with a new pot plant, cutting, or shrub.

Accordingly a new pair of hands was a godsend as far as he was concerned and he insisted then that Ernie continued his porter and booking office work at the same time as learning the signalbox. In truth he would probably have kept Ernie at the station all the time if he could. Rostering men for the signalbox was the responsibility of the District Inspector (D.I.), and therefore not his concern. It was amazing too how quickly he could forget, for Fred Parsons had been a permanent signalman himself at Sutton Scotney as well as taking up residence in the Station House. Just a few years earlier though, around 1942, he had successfully petitioned Paddington to restore the Station Master post – perhaps residing in the former station master's accommodation had given him the idea, but however this was achieved he was indeed promoted, after which time also the greeting "Fred" was no longer acceptable and he became known on the line as "Guvvy" Parsons. It was rumoured he had friends in high places, certainly such a promotion was considered unusual in wartime, at a time when there was already a shortage of skilled men working signalboxes.

Aside from Ernie and the "Guvnor", there was at this time another porter, Mr Turner, whilst later on, a "lad" was also employed. It was also the practice to play tricks on an unsuspecting new member of staff and so early on in his time at the station some of the older hands, perhaps including Ernie, sent the lad porter on an errand to collect supplies of red and green paraffin for the signal lamps. All this was watched with a detached interest by Mr Parsons, although when he felt the lad had searched enough he stopped the game with the words, "You've been had, laddie".

Whether the two ladies, Mrs Bird, and Miss Betty Allen, who had worked "on the platform" as it was called, during the war years had also been subject to such antics was not known to Ernie, although both had left the railway just before he started. Shortly

Signalman Arthur Watts – one of several men contemporary with Ernie, and one of those who also had a hand in training the new man. After a time "on the relief", Arthur settled down to be one of the regular men at Kings Worthy (the signalbox of which he is seen posed outside, sometime between 1948 and 1955). After 1955 and the closure of the signalbox here, he again went on the relief, often taking over from Ernie, or the other way around, at the varying shifts at Sutton Scotney.

(Courtesy Arthur Watts)

afterwards, probably around 1948, Jack Tanner arrived as a full time porter (believed as a replacement for Mr Turner), which quickly gave rise to the railway being known as the "seven-penny line", an understandable quip towards the surnames of Ernie and Jack.

The role of Porter, whether full or part time, was a bit inaccurate compared with the literal meaning of the actual title. Certainly there was the occasion when a passenger may have requested assistance with luggage on the platform, but most of the time the porters were involved in the general operation of the station. Accordingly it could be loading or unloading sacks in the goods yard, delivering goods locally on the station bicycle, entering details of all goods sent and received in the ledgers, working in the booking office, and of course general cleaning and tidying. They would also clean and fill the signal lamps on a weekly basis – but not with different coloured paraffin! As such there was always something to do – Mr Parsons saw to that as well!

But "Guvvy" could not keep Ernie away from the signalbox for ever, even though he may well have tried to tempt him with a life on the platform and the promise of perhaps promotion to Station Master at some time in the future. Years previous, a man wanting to be a

signalman spent years on the platform to begin with, passing first an internal correspondence course in signalling, the results of which would be posted also in the staff *Great Western Magazine*. Only after this could he hope to aspire to the bottom rung of the signalling ladder. Perhaps even Mr Parsons' reluctance was based partly on the traditions of the past, and partly on his fear of the amount of work that would be left.

Accordingly on September 8th 1947 Ernie joined the duty signalman, Rod McEntee on early turn and, after watching Rod deal with the first down train, it was over to Ernie to do the lot, and that probably involved making the tea at regular intervals as well. Today perhaps this may seem a bit unfair, but that was the way it was done then, and had indeed been done by generations of men who had been given a "strapper" to teach. (The term "strapper" was the general phrase applied to all trainees on the traffic department, and had also been so for generations. Its origins are believed to have been back in the days of the stagecoach, when the apprentice coachman's first task would be to climb onto the roof to strap the luggage down. Indeed if the Inspector enquired how a trainee was progressing, it would normally be, "How's the strapper doing?")

A rare survivor, and given to the author many years ago by Ernie Penny. The first entries for Ernie as a signalman at Sutton Scotney, showing his actions relative to down trains on the day he took on. (Up trains were recorded on the opposite side of the book.) Despite the thousands of mechanical signalboxes that once existed, and the countless Train Registers that were so studiously compiled, few have survived. Collectors often regarded these as of little consequence, and yet the history they reveal is often unique. Indeed, without the survival of the 1947 register, none of this text could ever have been written.

Bob Sullivan (always Mr Sullivan, never Bob to his face) would certainly have made enquiries from time to time as to Ernie's progress, hence Mr Parsons had to ensure he did not poach the new man too much. Incurring the wrath of the D.I. was something not even the Station Master would undertake lightly. Besides, the vacancy at Sutton Scotney that Ernie was hopefully going to fill was presently being tasked by one of Bob Sullivan's relief men, and they were urgently needed elsewhere, hence the regular enquiries made as to Ernie's progress.

Learning on the job was only one option to becoming a signalman, the alternative was to progress through the Reading Signal School although most men seemed to learn initially in the box where they were due to work, provided the D.I. also felt there was a good teacher available. In this then there was no formal training to teach a new man, it was down to experience, and the skill of the D.I. at recognising who was good as a tutor. A man could be an excellent signalman but no good at training others. Nowadays of course, companies spend thousands assessing, selecting and training individuals to be trainers. Back in the days of the GWR it was done locally and totally successfully as well, assuming of course you had a man like Bob Sullivan in charge. Of course there were also times when a man would be sent for training and the regular signalman would not let him near the levers so, when the time came for the D.I. to visit and pass him, he could quickly tell what had happened. Said "trainer" would never do it a second time!

So aside from actually learning the "pulls" – all signal and point levers require a different amount of effort, Ernie would have been coached in the Rules and Regulations as well. Likewise the rules for signalling trains on a single line under "Reg 4 – Line clear" and "Reg 5 (when authorised) – Line clear as far as home signal only", which applied to all the signalboxes on the branch south of Newbury but only for non-passenger trains. In addition there were the various actions to be taken in case of emergency, local instructions, the layout and gradients both at and either side of the station, as well as the actual train service, bell codes, physical operation of the equipment, maintenance, signal-box housekeeping and protocol. In addition there was a need to have an understanding of the set-up at the signalboxes on either side. A lot then to learn, followed potentially by years of repetition.

From surviving records, Ernie's training appears to have involved mainly early turns, whether this was through choice or otherwise is not certain, although one advantage was the opportunity to earn overtime in the afternoon working on the station. Although not "signing the book" as duty signalman, his neat handwritten entries in the Train Register are also in marked contrast to the almost illegible scrawl of some of his colleagues who worked the box on other shifts. Hence it is possible to work out on which days he was learning. His training appears to have continued for some three weeks, although there were also a number of days when he appears not to have been in the box – possibly "borrowed" then by Mr Parsons for what were considered more important tasks. One can almost imagine the words, "Come on Penny I need you today, you've been in that signalbox long enough."

But the spectre of Bob Sullivan was always in the background, and so it perhaps comes as no surprise to read that the signalbox Train Register records Bob Sullivans's signature as having visited at 3.00pm on Thursday 25th September, at which time he no doubt came to grill Ernie on the Rules as well as question him closely on the local instructions and finally watch him operate the frame.

In all these areas Ernie passed with flying colours, partly down to having a good teacher and partly, of course, down to being a studious learner; besides, who wanted to push a broom on the platform indefinitely? You could not pull the wool over the eyes of the D.I. either, as he knew the box inside out himself – that was his job, to know the workings of all the boxes and all the men in his district – a district that extended on the main line from Theale to Bedwyn, the branch from Upton and Blewbury down to Winchester, and also the Lambourn line as well.

If Ernie had perhaps got a little tongue-tied, Bob Sullivan might have eased up a bit, but not with the emergency bells, the rules for sending or receiving "6 – Emergency Line

The drivers eye view approaching Sutton Scotney from the direction of Worthy Down. The road bridge carries what is a minor road from Sutton Scotney village proper towards the village of Wonston and was also once used by agricultural traffic between the station and the village of Norton. The down gradient at this point approaching the station is also obvious. It was views such as this that a new signalman would be expected to gain for themselves and hence one of the reasons Ernie would walk to the signalboxes on either side as part of his learning process.

(Rodney Lissenden)

Obstructed" or "7 – Stop and Examine". These were expected to be recited without hesitation. Of course, Rod and Ernie would probably have had some prior warning of the D.I.'s arrival, the "bush telegraph", or more accurately in signalbox terms, the omnibus phone circuit, meaning that he would no doubt have been spotted either leaving Newbury or by one of the men at the stations he passed on the way down. Accordingly, the message that the D.I. was on the train would be a clear indication to all the men in all the boxes to make sure the book (Train Register) was up to date, the box tidy, and the kettle topped up.

Having successfully passed out at Sutton Scotney, Ernie was then expected to physically visit the signalboxes on either side as well. This was not written down in any regulation but just a common sense approach so that, as mentioned above, he could see at first hand the workings as applied there and how they might in turn then affect him at Sutton Scotney. Neither was this a simple "jump on the train" job either, he would be expected to walk, and in so doing observe for himself the sighting of his own signals as viewed from ground level. If he was lucky though he might get a lift back, on the footplate. This would be ideal, as Ernie had at one time considered a footplate career but quickly rejected this as it would mean moving away from his beloved village. The footplate return trip affording a true driver's eye view of the signals approaching his own station.

Accordingly Friday afternoon 26th September, was spent walking the three miles south to Worthy Down and then, on the Saturday, just over two miles north to Lodge Bridge, the latter the intermediate wartime block post perched high on an embankment, mid-way to Whitchurch.

Ernie was now ready to be on his own and that actually happened for the first time on Sunday 28th September when he opened the signalbox at 6.30am but for just an hour and a half in the morning ready for an Engineer's special, before closing again at 8.00am. He might really not have bothered opening until 7.00am, but he wanted time on his own to make sure everything was right, hence the earlier start. A split-shift that day meant a repeat of the work from 4.00pm and 5.00pm in the afternoon ready for the return of the Engineer's working – such trains were rarely late finishing those days, the men on them glad of the overtime but also glad to get home.

So Monday 29th September was his first full day. Booked for early turn, this would be Ernie's first day with a regular service. One of his former mentors, Rod McEntee (the other was Arthur Watts) would now be working opposite Ernie on the late turn, whilst Ron Hyde, who had previously been at Sutton Scotney was now back on the relief – possibly at Lodge Bridge where Bob Sullivan was having a difficult task finding regular men, not assisted by its inconvenient location.

Although he could not have known it at the time, Ernie was destined to spend 17 years at Sutton Scotney, and would have the melancholy distinction to be almost the last man on duty when the box and line finally closed in August 1964. Staying on the railway for a further two years, he transferred to Wallers Ash, south of Micheldever on the main Bournemouth line, until that signalbox too closed in 1966. After this came a spell with a garage in Winchester, although he was not happy there and moved back again to the railway, this time to the stores at Eastleigh. But despite being back with railwaymen again, it was never quite the same as when he had been in the signalbox. In this respect he was not alone either. The piecemeal closure of mechanical signalboxes in the 1960s associated with modern colour light signalling allied to railway closures meant dozens of men were in the same situation locally. He would though continue to live in the village, retiring there also, after which he became prominent in local affairs as well as tending to his garden.

In this respect, Ernie's working life was in reality little different to many others. Some might say it was to an extent an insular existence and lifestyle but that was how it had also been for countless previous generations in the local area. His though would perhaps also be the last generation to both originate from and remain living and working in the same area for almost all of that time. Indeed, had the railway survived, he would probably have remained "in-post" until retirement.

With the grateful thanks then to his surviving family, this is Ernie's railway story for the first 17 years of his working life. In many respects perhaps typical of countless others, but it must also be said, the story of a delightful man.

Sutton Scotney depicted in what was probably some time during the period August 1922 to January 1933. The tall man on the platform is believed to be the then Station Master, Mr Redman although the Porter standing next to him cannot be identified. Ernie would have recalled scenes such as this at a time before he joined the railway. The former ground frame hut seen in the view on page 4, has now been re-sited for parcel use at the rear of the platform. At the rear of the yard is the coal merchants office – probably that of Messrs Didhams.

(Tom Palmer courtesy Reg Harvey)

Chapter 2

A HURRIED START

With his canvas knapsack containing his breakfast over his shoulder, Ernie walked across the station yard just before 6.00am that morning. The station house, occupied by Mr Parsons the Sutton Scotney Station Master together with his wife Mrs Parsons was in darkness, and aside from what could well have been a fox scurrying across the shadows there was no sign of movement.

Fred Parsons was a singular man (his father had been Station Master here from 1898 to 1922), a former signalman, but unpredictable at times, and in some ways perhaps a bit of a martinet. Not in any way nasty, but you never knew where he would turn up next. One morning he had even startled Ernie by appearing from out of the shadows of the goods shed, his response being that he was checking the security of the site. "More like he was checking on me or had been chastised by Mrs Parsons", thought Ernie. All the staff thought that she ruled the roost at home, even if in public she generally seemed a shy creature.

Indeed days could go past without her apparently venturing outside the house. What she must get up to nobody could guess, but it must be said both were always immaculately turned out and probably the inside of the station house was the same. Not that anyone ever got to see inside that is, after all he was "management", and Ernie was "one of the rest". (An example of this was at meal times, when Mr Parsons would venture back indoors, leaving the platform staff to take their break in the former waiting room, a section of which was now given over to the porters.)

Fred Parsons would also certainly know if it had been a fox Ernie had seen, for he kept chickens at the end of his garden and with the tell tale signs of such a visit only too apparent from the trails of feathers left behind. The half light at that early hour also meant there were deep shadows in many areas, some hiding obstructions to trap the unwary, but Ern was made of sterner stuff, and it was with a certain assuredness that his boots crunched across the yard in the direction of his work place – the

signalbox – situated on the opposite side of the tracks.

Most days at this time the noise made by his own walking would be all that could be heard but today there was a different sound, a faint ringing, and which grew ever louder as he neared the running lines. Every other morning things had been quiet – just how he liked it, after all Ernie was the same as most of the populace and appreciated a gentle "coming to" at the start of the working shift where he could settle in at his own pace and in his own time.

With his feet crunching across the cinder and ash of the goods yard, Ernie continued on beneath the shadow of what was an empty coal wagon. A pair of box vans were also partly visible on the goods shed siding. Ernie knew only too well what they had contained, boxes of tinned food destined for the NAAFI canteen at nearby Barton Stacey army camp. He had been delegated to assist in their unloading, the squaddies sent for the task only too willing to sit smoking on the tail-board of their lorry, content to watch someone else do the task they had been suppose to undertake. Indeed, when Ernie protested to the Station Master the only response he got was to the effect of, "What the army does is up to them, but the railway need that wagon back in use, so you just get on and unload it". It was pointless arguing further.

That morning, the route Ernie took across the yard was also the furthest from the station, keeping close to Didhams' Coal Merchants office rather than the goods shed. To do otherwise could risk waking Mr Parsons. Ernie well remembering the occasion one morning when he had walked along the platform, thus passing the station house, ready to go on early shift – only to be chastened later for making too much noise and waking him or her up – Ernie could not remember which one had seemingly been disturbed. And it did not seem to make much difference if there was a light on either.

"Perhaps they sometimes left the light on all night, or got up without putting one on even", he mused to himself. Accordingly, the furthest distance from the main building was the safest route and so that was naturally the course that was chosen. (Another reason for the light being left on might have been the novelty of electricity as the station house was only connected to the mains supply as recently as June 1945.)

That morning though, as he neared the running lines, the sound was more distinct – the dreaded telephone. The single long ring, which made the railway telephone system so different from that of the GPO. The sound punctuated by a momentary pause and then another long ring, getting louder and louder as he approached. All this despite the fact that all the windows and the door of the box were firmly closed.

Instinctively also, Ernie glanced along the tracks before crossing them. Logic could have told him that there could not be anything about at that time, but it was a habit he and every other railwayman possessed, and certainly a practice few would forget in a hurry. Reaching the door he felt under the step for the key. This was hidden under a large concrete slab provided as a doorstep, which was also supported at the corners so allowing space underneath. It was then but a moment to open the door and replace the key, the sound of the telephone suddenly loud, its urgent ring almost demanding immediate attention.

With the door open the smell was also immediate and obvious, a not unpleasant mixture of oil, paraffin, brasso and floor polish, such smells commonplace in signalboxes everywhere, so much so that the regular men became immune in much the same way as a baker soon fails to notice the smell of fresh bread. With the light by now also switched on, normally Ernie would have climbed the stairs at his regular pace, but something this time made him act faster and if anyone had been watching they would have seen him climb several steps two at a time. It was but a few seconds more to reach the upstairs operating floor and finally stop the offending noise by grabbing at the handset.

"Sutton Scotney," he blurted out, not even following protocol of listening to see if anyone was going to talk first.

"Ah, you are there," came the voice from the other end, "and about blooming time as well."

Ernie was about to comment that he was not officially on duty until 6.00am and it was then only 5.55am but he was stopped in mid sentence by hearing the words,

"Whitchurch here, Ken speaking, now listen. The down goods from Didcot is running early and it's waiting at my starter. Lodge Bridge has been trying to reach you as well but the boy there didn't know what to do so as he couldn't get a reply, so I'm trying for him. Anyway, the goods has some urgent vans for Eastleigh and there is also that truck load of coal for you as well, the one they couldn't find for a couple of days. Seems someone misread the label and it ended up at Steventon. Anyway it's on the goods and he's going to put it off on the way. So hurry up and switch in, it's blooming noisy with an engine outside here at this hour."

With that the phone went dead.

Ken at Whitchurch might well have received this information direct from Newbury Exchange, Whitchurch being the nearest manned signalbox to Sutton Scotney. Strictly speaking of course Lodge Bridge was nearer, but with a junior working the place, Newbury probably felt – or even found out, it was safer to leave the important message elsewhere. Other times information would be passed "box to box" so to speak, and was invariably prefaced by comment on various news issues or local gossip, although there was always the risk that an important message could become distorted having travelled through a number of men. (Ken had also decided to keep the train with him at Whitchurch even though he could by rights have sent it forward to Lodge Bridge. The fact that the signalman at Lodge Bridge was of limited experience meant it was better to control matters where he could see them.)

Having finished his last shift as the late turn man on Saturday, and with no trains that Sunday, Sutton Scotney signalbox was in the same condition as when Ernie had left it, the duster across the levers, and numbers 7, 16, 17 and 18 reversed. This meant that the motor points at the end of the loop were set in the straight position. These four levers reversed meaning that the running line was lined up for a through route and in the event of a runaway occurring elsewhere it would have a straight run through the station and not derail itself or

The station yard area as would have been seen my Ernie first thing in the morning. The signalbox is just out of sight to the left of the goods shed as is the long siding where coal wagons would be berthed.   *(Ernie Penny)*

run into stationary vehicles somewhere in the yard. Again it was not written in any rule book that the line should be left as such, just good practice, handed down from one man to the next. Ernie knew also that for his first few days or even weeks as a signalman Mr Parsons would be keeping a close eye on proceedings, especially to make sure there were no delays that could be attributable to him.

"Guvvy" (Parsons) was not a bad man at all, but he did like everything to run smoothly and not affect his own quintessentially eccentric activities, which seemingly revolved around the floral display of the station garden, his own position in the village, and lastly the operation of "his" station. So far though, things had been fine, the few weeks since Ernie had "took on" having passed with remarkable speed and up to now, without incident. Being disturbed by the phone at that time of the morning though was not a good start.

"Arrive early, not even six o'clock, and pestered by Whitchurch before there is even time to settle in first" he mused. "Well, there are such things as priorities and the first is to light the stove and get the kettle on."

It may not have been strictly necessary to light a fire, after all the day had started dry and the forecast was for it to remain the same, so the fire was not really needed. But the down side of this was how would he otherwise boil a kettle? There was then no option and so with a single match the prepared paper and wood were quickly burning – the coal would catch soon afterwards.

After that came the requisite communication with Lodge Bridge to "open" the signalbox, officially belled as "five-pause-five-pause-five", which was immediately acknowledged back. Then there was the "testing" phase, this time 16 rings on the bell, which was again repeated by each man, who also tested to see that a token could be released – no problem there. All being well, this was immediately followed by the goods being offered to him as a code "one-four" on the block bell – really a "block gong" as the sound was relayed though a gong encased on three sides and top by a polished wooden frame. A conventional block bell was provided though for communication with Worthy Down.

"Should be "one-two" as a branch freight if he is dropping one off here", Ernie thought to himself, but to be fair this was an exception to drop off a wagon from what was normally a through service and as everyone involved knew what was happening no harm was done.

SUTTON SCOTNEY (1943)

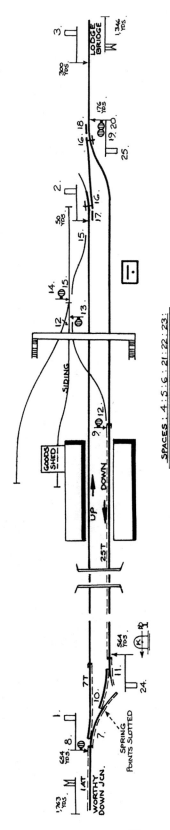

SPACES : 4 : 5 : 6 : 21 : 22 : 23 :

GWR TYPE 13 SIGNAL BOX, 24' 2" X 12' ELEVATED 8'.
OPENED 06-11-1942 AS REPLACEMENT FOR BOX ON
PREVIOUS PAGE (EXTENDED LOOP FOR WAR
TRAFFIC)
VT 5-BAR FRAME, 4" CENTRES.
FPLs STAND NORMALLY "OUT".
POINTS 7, 10 & 11 WORKED BY MOTOR (HAND
GENERATOR).
ELECTRIC KEY TOKEN.
CLOSING SWITCH:- NIL.

(The "one-pause-two" bell code, was also universally used by the men communicating with each other by the bells and asking the next man to pick up the telephone – it saved ringing out long codes on the omnibus phone.)

In the quiet of the morning, Ernie could imagine the sound of the gong carrying for some distance and so disturbing many of the villagers, although in practice it would be unlikely to be heard by many.

Usually a signalman could tell if a regular or relief man was on duty at the signalbox that he worked to on either side, simply by the way the bells were rung. Some men were slow and deliberate, whilst others banged the whole lot in one go to make it appear like a continuous cacophony of sound. The trick was to know what to expect – something his mentor Rod had instilled into him early on. For example, Ernie knew the sum total of bells initially should be 15 beats even if sometimes the sound that came through was indeed in rapid succession with no apparent gaps between. This was in fact commonplace, gaps between the codes in reality difficult to determine to the untrained ear although in practice they were usually there even if only very briefly. If a code was ever sent in a long string then it was either a relief man (they always seemed to do everything in a hurry) or something else was urgently in need of attention – like a boiling kettle!

At this stage Ernie then turned to the Train Register and started making his entries. Writing across one side of the page, he started with the date and then added "Box opened at 5.55 am".

Ernie's entries in the all important Train Register were some of the neatest and most legible of all the men who worked the signalbox. But as he rested his forearm on the desk, having completed the bookwork, he had two thoughts: firstly, would the next signalbox south, Worthy Down, likewise be early in opening? and second, where in the approaching train was the wagon that had to be put off at his station? It took but a few moments to ascertain the latter from a by now somewhat more relaxed Ken Alexander at Whitchurch, with the simple answer that it was the first vehicle immediately behind the engine's tender.

Now, no signalman would ever dream of offering spontaneous advice to a colleague, and

Ken was no exception. But the fact that Ernie had asked a question invoked a suggested response. It was no more than one man acknowledging the position and authority of another, but without interfering, after all they were all GWR men and as such respected each other's position. The boy at Lodge Bridge was another matter altogether. (This bleak signalbox just controlled a passing loop mid way between Whitchurch and Sutton Scotney, north of where Barton Stacey Halt had once stood. It had only been in existence since 1942 and simply passed trains from one signalbox to another with no sidings or station thereabouts. The trouble was, nobody wanted to work it either and a succession of young men had been posted there but they rarely stayed longer than a few weeks, hence relief men were also used. Who could blame the youngsters either? It was a lonely spot, miles from anywhere and meaning the poor lad either had to lodge locally – if he could find somewhere that is, or be faced with a long cycle ride each end of the shift. Small wonder then that the latest new lad had panicked when he could not raise Ernie earlier on.)

With the information from Ken in his mind, Ernie had to think quickly, after all Ken's demeanour meant the train had by now left Whitchurch southwards and would be on its way to Lodge Bridge. Any moment now Lodge Bridge would also be putting it "On line" and Ernie would then be committed. Accordingly he quickly restored levers 17 and 16 to normal before pulling number 18, which would allow the train to run into the down line as normal. The final requirement was to change the motor points at the far end, which he did with the use of levers 11 and 7, and the associated hand generator.

The question was, how best to split the train so the wagon could be shunted into the yard? And, if in the opinion of the driver he got it wrong, there would be hell to pay as well! The obvious means was to bring the whole train into the down platform, run the engine around, and then pull the train back towards Lodge Bridge before shunting forward to push the single wagon into its place by the coal staiths. Next, the whole train would have to be pushed back into the platform, the engine uncoupled and run around again so it was at the correct

Freight working on the railway near to Lodge Bridge, north of Sutton Scotney, probably around 1951. The service is probably that of empty coal wagons originating from Winchester Gas Works.
(J F Russell-Smith / National Railway Museum)

end before departure to Worthy Down. All this could take some considerable time, more if the crew considered they were being made to work more than necessary – it was certainly not unknown for a driver to deliberately prevaricate it he was feeling particularly stubborn.

Another, perhaps easier, solution was to halt the train by the signalbox, or even on the single line on the approach to the station, and then uncouple the first wagon and just get the crew to push it back into the headshunt via the trailing crossover into the goods yard. This was a lot more simple and a lot quicker, but it would mean the wagon would not only be at the wrong end of the yard but, being full as well, it would be almost impossible to shift later with just pinch-bars and muscle power. Possibly though, the coalman might not mind using his horse to pull it with a rope again but that would put him in bad mood and he would no doubt take it up with Mr Parsons as well.

Ernie could well imagine the Station Master's reaction, "Now look here Penny, the customer is important, and I don't care what the driver said, your job is to tell him where *you* want him to put the wagon, not where he wants to put it, understand?"

It was alright though for the Guvnor, he would not be around whilst this was going on. Strange wasn't it how the boss always seemed to be absent at times like these? But there again, that was why he was the boss. Looked after his own little area and beggar everywhere else. He didn't have to face the wrath from Control at Reading when things went wrong and were delayed. And that usually precipitated a visit from Bob Sullivan, the Newbury D.I. at some stage as well.

Two solutions then to the same problem, neither of which were ideal, the situation compounded by the fact that, at that precise moment, 6.10am, came two beats on the bell from Lodge Bridge, meaning the train was on the way and now no more than about six to seven minutes away. Probably if Ernie had opened the north end window to the signalbox he might even have heard it approaching through the still morning air as indeed he

14

sometimes did, but not today, there was no time, and he still had to think.

Insofar as the rules were concerned Ernie had everything ready for the train. The lock on points 16 (lever 18) was reversed and so Ernie could, if he wished, lower his home signal, No 25, to allow the goods to enter the station normally. For the section south, he had also managed to rouse Worthy Down slightly early, first tapping out a single beat on the brass plunger of the token instrument at the south, or station end, of the signalbox. This was likewise repeated back as a further single beat to the cow bell located on the instrument shelf. After this, Ernie again picked up his duster and sent the necessary five-five-five on the bell, which was similarly acknowledged. He now sent 16 beats in rapid succession, holding down the brass plunger of the bell push on the very last beat and at the same time watching until the associated galvanometer needle on the token machine flicked briefly. This meant Worthy Down had successfully obtained a token for test purposes and was now probably checking he could pull his own starting signal. He could now only wait until the token was replaced at the other end.

It was not long. A single beat on the Worthy Down bell corresponded with the galvanometer needle again flicking across and remaining at an angle. This was Ernie's cue, and even before the sound of the bell had totally died away, a quick flick had enabled him to release a token from the machine. Moving now to the lever frame, he released the catch on lever No 24, at the same time pressing the brass release plunger above the lever, which was itself labelled 24. Almost instantaneously, there was a single click from deep in the bowels of the locking room that indicated the lock had "picked" and which similarly meant the lever could be moved slightly out of the frame and the plunger released.

Ernie could now apply all his strength to pulling the lever towards him and as he did so he released the catch handle, so allowing the catch at the bottom to slide across the metal quadrant. At the end of quadrant the catch now dropped into place, thus leaving No 24 reversed in the frame. Ernie simultaneously checked on the Bakelite repeater that the arm

had indeed responded. (A repeater was provided as the signal was out of his sight, beyond the road bridge.) The little needle of the repeater seemed to remain obstinately pointing to the On position, but after a second moved across to the right before falling back and then finally settling against the right hand pin in its required Off position. Observing this, Ernie pulled the lever slightly towards him and again squeezed the catch to release it so allowing the tension of the signal wire to carry the lever back to its correct place in the frame. At the same time the thought went through his mind of the words his former mentor had told him the first time he had attempted to put a signal lever back to its "normal" position:

"Never let it go back on its own – always guide it, if you don't the wire can come off its pulley and that means more work for you."

Ernie could now return the token to its position in the machine and wait to receive 16 bells from Worthy Down – test concluded!

As he had expected, the phone also rang straight away. This time it was Ron Fisher at Worthy Down, also sounding slightly annoyed at being disturbed earlier than normal. He though quickly regained his composure once the circumstances were explained. Indeed, as Ron saliently pointed out:

"Trouble is, the goods is due to cross with the first up passenger here anyway (meaning at Worthy Down), and if you delay it with your shunt, either he will be late getting here and the passenger will then be delayed, or you will have to cancel the goods and I will offer you on the passenger anyway."

It was not ideal; Ernie was stuck in the middle, with the goods approaching ever nearer by the minute.

The official timetable showed the goods and passenger were due to cross at Worthy Down, the Goods due to arrive at 7.07am and then scheduled to wait for the passenger service, which was due at Worthy Down at 7.17am, although, in practice, the goods ran at a slightly different time every day. Ernie had been warned of this during his learning of the box for the time when he would "take on" on his own.

As Arthur Watts had once told him when he had been watching Ernie learn Sutton Scotney:

Ernie in characteristic signalman's pose. From this position he could reach the single line token from the fireman as the engine passed, although such action from the signalbox was frowned upon by officialdom – the rationale being that the token could easily swing back and break a window.

(Ernie Penny)

"Trouble with the morning goods is that it is scheduled to leave Didcot at 4.15am with two engines, one of which drops off at Newbury as the pilot. But getting two engines prepared and ready to leave at the same time can be a problem. The crews will be there, but if Didcot shed is busy and they cannot get one out 'cause something else is in the way, or they cannot get coal or water then the train will leave late.

"Depends on the load as well, it might be a lot or a little. The weather also does not help. As this is the first train for some hours the rails can be greasy and he might then take longer up the banks than usual. Or one of the signalman farther up the line might be late. Having said that sometimes it all goes well and he runs early, you just never know.

"Never understood why he's not booked to cross the passenger at Kings Worthy, even if he just sticks to the timetable he could make that easily. When I'm working Kings Worthy we sometimes run him on so he does cross there. Trouble is, the Didcot crew don't always want to go that far, as they are due to swap over with Winchester men and if they go too far south that means they have to work further back as well. Depends on the crew, you will have to watch them, but you will get to know the regulars after a while."

With Worthy Down then open, Ernie had all areas covered, well almost, and if they did get a move on with the shunt, the train could be on its way immediately, although in practice, by the time the manoeuvre was complete, this was unlikely to be much before the booked time anyway.

Again, the entries in the Train Register to show "Open to Worthy Down" were made, but as he put down the pen again Ernie paused. An idea was formulating, perhaps not strictly legal but one that would certainly help the situation. A slight bit of rule bending, not in any way dangerous as such, but certainly contrary to what Bob Sullivan, would officially approve of.

Grabbing his duster, Ernie pushed back the FPL, No 18, and instead pulled points No 16, followed again by the FPL No 18. In so doing, he set the road directly this time for a down train to work "wrong-road" (sometimes it was referred to as "bang-road"), into the up platform. He would attend to the motor points at the far end later. This action was strictly against the rules insofar as he had moved points 16 in the face of an oncoming train and in as much as the set of points in question were within the 440 yard "clearing point" ahead of the down home signal. Regulation 4 clearly stated that, before a train is accepted there must be a minimum 440 yards clear, ahead of the home signal, which was intended to allow a safety margin in the event of an over-run. Indeed, once a train had been accepted under Regulation 4, the signalman was forbidden to move any points within that 440 yard clearing point until the train had come to a stop.

In his defence of course, Ernie would state

that the home signal had been at danger throughout, it would have been a different matter if he had pulled this to the Off position and then put it back On as would have been necessary to reset the road. In addition, the train would also be expecting to stop and not run straight through, so no-one would ever know what had happened. Actually, unbeknown to Ernie there was one witness, but he would never say anything – a small brown rabbit disturbed from its foraging in the nearby embankment by the squeal and screech of the point rodding that passed only a few inches from where it had been grazing.

The next stage was for Ernie to leave the signalbox and make his way as quickly as possible to the home signal, No 25, the train likely to be arriving within a minute or two. Indeed, as he made his way along the ash path to the signal he could already see the engine approaching.

As he waited, his mind went back to a few weeks earlier when, as a learner, he had answered the phone one Monday morning with "Sutton Scotney", only to be hear the words:

"Mornin', just to start the week right, the 4.15am had to put off one at Burghclere with a hot-box. He's moving again now though, engine crew seem intent on making up time – probably them daft beggars caused the hot box in the first place by running too fast anyway. Should be with you in about 15 minutes, right?"

"Yes, thank you", replied Ernie and replaced the receiver, only then realising he had not found out who it was who was passing the message to him in the first place!

He would not make that mistake again. Cursing himself he had even though of calling his neighbour at Lodge Bridge, but quickly dismissed the idea. He could not even be certain it was Lodge Bridge that had called!

On that occasion a decision had to be made, and together with his mentor the easiest choice was simply to wait until "it was offered" and then choose whether to let it run or hold it for the first up passenger to arrive. The latest they could afford to wait being about 6.55am so as not to delay the train in the opposite direction. As it was, the goods did not finally make an appearance until the chimes of the church clock nearby were marking 7.00am.

Both trains then crossed at his station that morning, contrary to the timetable of course, but as he learned, just one example of the type of decisions that would need to be made almost on a daily basis. It was all good experience and one in which he learned the priority was invariably the passenger service, and the more important the passenger service, the more priority it received. (Prioritising hardly applied on the minor routes, but it did apply on main lines and at junctions, which could have a knock-on effect with the branch line services.)

As he reflected on the past, Ernie was still carefully watching the approaching goods train as well. He had seen the engine clearly before the driver saw him, as a column of steam broke the calm of the dawn sky to be followed a moment later by the shrill screech of an engine whistle.

"Beggar hasn't seen me," thought Ernie, "thinks I'm asleep and forgot to lower the signal. Bet he thinks he is going to put the wagon off in the headshunt as well."

Possibly this was indeed what had been going through the mind of the driver, although by now he had ceased his whistling as Ernie had crossed to the far side of the track and so would have been seen by the driver who was leaning out of the cab as the train approached. Engine and signalman arrived at the same spot simultaneously, Ernie craning his head towards the cab although as he did the driver turned in for a moment and obviously speaking to his fireman commented:

"Shut the feed off for a moment mate, I can't hear the man here."

Clearly obeying the command there was a brief gurgle and a phut, after which all that was left was a quiet simmering and the occasional sound of dripping water. The driver was the first to speak,

"What's up mate, thought you'd run us straight in, I can drop 'im off in the headshunt."

"Trying it on as I thought he would", Ernie said to himself, but instead he looked up and responded:

"No, I've a better idea. I've set the road for the up line, so leave the rest of the train here, come forward with the one wagon, drop him off between the loop and the yard points and then run round. You can then push the

What is probably the 12.40pm up freight off Winchester (destined for Newbury racecourse, the times also varied slightly over the years), due at Sutton Scotney between 1.53 and 2.09pm. This service would then shunt the yard as required, collecting wagons for onward transit as well as dropping off full loads. Communication between the signalboxes for this service would be "one-pause-two".

(Derek Cross)

wagon in then straight back onto your train and away."

"Nay," responded the driver, "Much quicker to do it my way."

"The other way it is driver," responded Ernie, "I'll go back and give you the dummy," and without allowing further discussion he turned on his heel and commenced his walk back to the box.

What was being thought or even said on the footplate was probably rather less than polite at this stage, and if he had waited the next comment would no doubt have been to try and pressure him on the basis that some the rest of the vans were needed at Eastleigh urgently. But so was the coal needed urgently here, and that was more, local to his own location. Eastleigh would have to wait – besides that was the Southern. (He could not have imagined that, within a few short years, Sutton Scotney would be part of what would then be the Southern Region of British Railways.)

Now, at this stage it might be considered that, bearing in mind the urgency of the situation, which involved getting the train on its way as soon as possible as well as not delaying the first up passenger service, Ernie might have been inclined to run back to the box. After all, he was fit – several years in the army had seen to that, and to run the 180 odd yards would have taken no more than few seconds. Instead though he walked, a brisk but steady pace, reflective of the man in charge; he would not be hurried nor pressured.

Having arrived back at the signalbox he first pulled lever No 19, which cleared the dummy (ground-disc signal), allowing the engine to draw forward with its solitary wagon. To do this of course the driver would first have had to instruct his fireman to apply the brake on the second and perhaps next few wagons of the train and then wait for his mate to uncouple between the first and second wagons. Clearly though during the time it had taken to walk back to the box, the driver had also accepted Ernie's demands, for immediately the disc came off there was a brief toot from the engine and Ernie was now at the window ready with a

Ernie retrieving the token from the set down post just north of the station. Despite the recognised belief in Great Western "standardisation", the set down post at Sutton Scotney for down trains was backed with a horsehair filled pouch compared with the more usual mesh rope surrounded by a metal frame. The set down post still survives today, although now at the home of the Great Western Society, Didcot.

red flag. Engine and wagon came to a stop in the gap between the loop points (16) and catch point (16). After this, Ernie made sure the driver had seen his red flag before turning inside again to ring "one-two" on the omnibus phone to Worthy Down, which was answered almost immediately by Ron Fisher:

"Ron, we're doing alright here, the engine is just running round and after that he'll be off again straight away. How's the passenger doing?"

"Typical," came the reply, "all that hurry up we have to do and he hasn't even left Winchester yet, something about the fireman oversleeping."

"OK mate," replied Ernie, "talk to you on the bells in a minute.", and with that he replaced the receiver.

Next he walked to one of the three short levers in the frame (numbers 7, 10, and 11 controlled the south exit from the loop, and were all operated by electric motors due to their distance away) and pushed No 11 back from its reverse position to the notch in the treads of the frame. He now turned to the hand generator and began to turn the motor so as to supply power to the electric points. "Don't fail me this morning", he thought, a reminder of the time a week or so ago when the damn things had stuck just as he had been offered the last down passenger train, which of course had to coincide with a prolonged rain shower. It was a

rather bedraggled and not at all happy signalman who eventually returned to the signalbox swinging the hand crank necessary to operate the points from the ground after the quarter-mile trip to the end of the loop and then back again. To compound it all, his swinging of the heavy steel handle had been a bit too vigorous as he got back to the signalbox, with the result that one of the glass panels in the door had got broken. There had been a lot of explaining to do over that, but it was eventually accepted that the wind had probably caught the door and banged it shut causing the glass to break. After all, these things happened, just lucky that no-one remembered there was a bristle mat immediately inside that the door that the door had to be pushed against – hard!

But returning to today, as recounted earlier, when he had arrived at work that morning, the "road" had been left as he had set it with the motor points straight. He had then moved them so as to be able to test the starting signal for Worthy Down. Now, of course, it was necessary to restore them once more to the state they were in at the start! Ideally a signalman always tried to have everything ready in advance of the next movement, but that was only possible if trains worked to the timetable, this morning they did not. Sutton Scotney was also unusual of the stations on the line south of Newbury in that the loop did not have a straight run in and a curved exit.

Southbound trains had to take a curved path both in and out. That was the way it had been done since 1885, and even the rebuilding in 1943 did not alter matters and it would not change for the rest of the life of the line.

With the position of the south end points then changed, Ernie now went to the window again but this time raising his arm to indicate to the driver it was clear to proceed south. This was again acknowledged with a similar action from the man on the footplate, which was followed by a hiss and sucking noise and then an immediate bark as Didcot based 22xx No 2289 set off south with the brisk acceleration so typical of the type.

The use of a hand signal rather than a green flag should be explained at this stage: simply, a green flag covered the meaning of a signal that had failed, and indicated that it was safe to proceed. An arm signal on the other hand indicated it was clear to proceed in the required direction where there was no signal provided to cover the move. This was certainly the case here, as understandably there was no signal provided to allow a movement in the down (wrong) direction along the length of the up platform. By indicating with his hand, Ernie was informing the driver it was now safe to proceed to the far end of the loop. Regardless of his personal preference for where to deposit the wagon, this type of arm-signal message would have been clearly understood by the driver as well.

Ernie watched the engine for a minute and then returned to the frame. Restoring No 19 to normal he did likewise with numbers 18 and 16 and so prepared the road ready for the engine to run back and around the wagon. The engine by now had disappeared under the bridge at the far end of the platform, at which point Ernie turned his attention to the three black cased track-circuit repeaters that stood vertically, one above the other, at the left-hand end of the frame. (Wherever possible, the levers and indicators mirrored the position of the actual equipment on the ground. Hence the token instruments were positioned at the respective north and south ends of the signalbox, with the track-circuit repeaters similarly placed.)

Within a few moments the indicator at the top (track-circuit 7T) swung from its normal angle of "Track Clear" to "Track Occupied",

the indicator for No 1AT doing likewise, after which No 7T returned to "Track Clear". By this, Ernie knew the engine had cleared the points although, almost as confirmation, there were three distant toots on the whistle as a message from the driver that the engine was indeed clear.

"He'll be popular with that," thought Ernie, after all it was still only just after 6.30am and in some ways he was slightly surprised that Mr Parsons had so far seemingly not ventured out onto the platform, just to see what was going on.

It was now time to turn the motor points again, which was once more accomplished without difficulty. The wrong road working meant that the generator had to be used on no less than three separate occasions. Firstly to restore No 7, then to pull No 10, and finally No 11. After this, with relief in his mind, he could pull (reverse) No 8, which was the ground signal at the far end of the loop, allowing the engine to run back along the down platform – but of course in the up direction. Again Ernie watched the track circuit repeaters, 1AT and 7T together, then as 1AT returned to "Track Clear", 7T alone showed "Track Occupied", moments later to be joined by 25T: when this finally alone showed "Track Occupied" it confirmed to Ernie that the engine was indeed well on its way back.

With the knowledge all was proceeding well out of his sight, he made his way down the stairs and outside to catch the token from the fireman for the section from Lodge Bridge. (Ernie could very well have collected this from the driver at the time of their discussion earlier, likewise prior to giving his arm signal to proceed. It was purely choice on his part.) Again this showed the way the men, albeit from differing departments, worked together when necessity came to the fore. The fireman was ready to give up the token to Ernie, who leant out of the window as the engine went past. The loco was loosing speed all the time as it made its way back towards the waiting wagons that stood behind the home signal.

Upon returning to the signalbox, Ernie quickly removed the single line token from the carrier and placed it in the slot in the Lodge Bridge section token machine. For the moment though, he did not restore it into the instrument;

Eastleigh based 76019 paused at Sutton Scotney in the latter years of freight operation. Despite the variation in period of the photograph compared with the present chapter, little would have altered over the years. Indeed, in some respects, it could almost be said to be a return to older times as, even though the station and route as far as Newbury now came under the Southern Region, this series of Eastleigh based engines were then under the charge of just a single crew – a return to old times indeed. The head-code is that of a through freight, no doubt destined for Eastleigh.

after all, there might not be anything due, but the majority of the down goods was still outside the home signal in the single line section, and by restoring the token he would have been leaving the opportunity to release another token for a section that was still occupied. Instead, he obtained the token for the line south to Worthy Down and placed this in the token carrier ready to give to the driver shortly. He then restored No 8 to normal, but for the present did not use the generator again to move the motor points. There were two reasons for this, firstly the time it would take – he could do this when the actual shunt into the yard was taking place, and in any event he would probably have been prevented from doing so by the timer (a big glass case containing a clock-type mechanism that prevented the points being moved twice within a short period.) It was an extra safeguard in the working but on occasions such as this could also be a nuisance.

With the engine then seen to be clear of the north end loop points – this was easy from signalbox, he could pull No 15 to allow entry into the yard, then numbers 16 and 18, and finally the ground disc No 20, which allowed the engine to move slowly forward and buffer up again to the waiting wagon. By this time, Ernie had noticed the Guard of the goods was also waiting on the ground, ready to couple the wagon to the front of the engine, obviously having by now walked up from his van at the rear of the train.

"Move the yard points will you to put the wagon over the far side." called Ernie to him.

"Right-oh" came the response in a strong Berkshire accent, and it seemed then no time before the Guard had worked the necessary magic with his shunting pole, taken off the wagon brake, and was then walking slowly forward with the wagon, ready to ensure the coal was positioned exactly where it should be.

"Lucky the siding's almost empty as well." thought Ernie, "He (meaning the driver) would have been even less happy if there were other things in his way."

What Ernie could not have known was that, a couple of days before, Mr Parsons had ensured space was available in anticipation of the wagon arriving – as indeed it should have on that day. He had even cajoled the coal merchant to use his horse to shift the NAAFI vans further south along the goods shed siding so the way was clear for the coal anyway. At the time, the Station Master's demeanour was such that he almost persuaded the coalman that it was his duty to assist, and that it was the Station Master who was doing him a favour! The fact the wagon did not arrive was subsequently passed back to the coalman in the form that it was the coalman's fault as he had probably not ordered it early enough. You had to get up very early indeed to get one over on the Station Master. In practice at Sutton Scotney, the goods yard was really busy only at certain times of the year anyway, and even then, or as now when something needed shifting, everyone mucked in and helped each other anyway.

At this point in the proceedings, the engine was moving the wagon forward at only a very slow walking pace, the driver seemingly aware that here, as at many of the wayside yards of the branch, the yard trackwork was, to say the least, not up to running line standards. (Further north, that at Highclere was probably worst of all.) The running lines and loops had received much attention a few years before consequent upon the wartime improvements, but little had been done to several of the sidings, and minor derailments were a not infrequent result.

Again now wagon and engine almost disappeared from view, the driver consciously not fly shunting the vehicle, probably out of respect for the track. (Fly shunting was, as the name implies, pushing an uncoupled wagon hard and then braking the engine equally hard. The wagon would then go sailing off to stop, or be stopped, hopefully where it was required. Whilst an amount of time could be thus be saved with this method of working, it was strictly frowned upon.)

Matters were now out of Ernie's hands for a moment, and so he could turn his attention

back to the lever frame. It was a question of restore disc No 20 to normal and instead pull numbers 17 (the FPL for 16), 14 and then 2, which allowed the engine to exit the yard and back onto its train. He could then turn his attention to the motor points (setting these as usual for the departure of a down train – restore No 10 and have just No 11 reversed). He completed this action just as the engine slowly moved back out of the yard, ready to re-couple onto the main train, now minus the one wagon. It was now 6.37am and Ernie noticed that the guard was riding on the steps of the engine.

With the engine back against its train again, it was now time to restore levers number 2, 14, 16 and 17 to normal in the frame, before pulling over to the reverse position numbers 18, 24 and 25. The last two were the home and starting signals, which the driver would pass once he had re-coupled to the train, the wagon brakes had been taken off, and the Guard had rejoined his van.

The trouble was, this time the train seemed in no hurry to move. Ernie had not noticed the Guard or Fireman re-couple the engine to the train but this could well have been achieved on the far side, away from his view. In addition, the Guard would have had more than enough time by now to walk back to his van. He could almost imagine his telephone ringing again at any moment. Worthy Down calling perhaps to say the up passenger was off Kings Worthy – it could not continue to Sutton Scotney as the single line token had been released ready for the goods to go south, or control at Reading having received a message from Shawford Junction to enquire why the goods, which was supposed to have been arriving early, was not yet offered. It would give the Southern men some more ammunition to their regular claim about the Western in general and the DNS in particular, "Off the timetable and on to the calendar", a somewhat cryptic reference to the supposed running of trains to or from GWR lines.

There was absolutely nothing Ernie could do now. He had the token out, the signals were off, and there was no obvious reason why the train was not moving. The minutes passed. Glancing at the clock for what was probably the tenth time in just a few minutes, the hands had moved to just after ten minutes to seven. It hardly seemed possible, the engine had been standing there for over ten minutes and Ernie was almost considering venturing out to see what was going on, when a shuffle and a bark from the exhaust heralded the sign that the train was finally at last moving. Reaching for the token for the single line to Worthy Down, he went to the front window, slid it back, and held the big steel loop out ready for the fireman to collect as they went past. Still the engine was only travelling slowly although, after what seemed an age, it eventually came near enough for the token to be grabbed by the Fireman.

This afforded Ernie a glimpse onto the footplate, which immediately revealed the reason for the reluctant start. "The beggars were having tea" he mused, smiling slightly to himself as he considered for a moment the driver standing with one hand on the regulator and the other holding a tea cup. Another tea cup was perched somewhat precariously on top of the shelf above the fire door, Ernie able to witness the young fireman showing the token to the driver, who in turn glanced at it, before both resumed their tea drinking poses.

Ernie was also subconsciously counting the wagons as they passed, "25-30-35-38 and a van, must have been quite a struggle on some of the banks" he thought. The last vehicle was the van with the Guard standing on the veranda, he too with tea cup in hand; he at least did acknowledge the signalman with a wave.

Turning to the token instrument, Ernie, could now ring out two beats on the bell as "Train on line" to Worthy Down, before restoring No 25 and then sending "two-pause-one" to Lodge Bridge as "Train out of section" to that signalbox. (He had of course to wait to see the tail lamps on the van before sending "Train on line".) It was 6.53am so he entered this time into the respective columns of the Train Register, finally watching as the track circuit repeaters described the progress of the train south, which could also be followed by an increasing steam cloud in the morning air. The last act at this stage was to return No 25 and then No 24 to normal, and then set the road ready for the up passenger – whenever it would arrive that is (officially 7.24am).

Finally he could attend to his kettle, almost dry by that time, but of course easily topped up. As he did so though he again paused to think. Yes, he had broken one rule with regards to the clearing point, but it was dawning on him that he had also broken another – allowing the light engine to proceed beyond the down starting signal for the purpose of running round before he had obtained the token for that section. True, there was no token out for a train approaching either, but he realised he should not have allowed the move without either having first obtained a token, or alternatively sending "Shunting into forward section" to Worthy Down. The driver could not have known this to be the case. He would put his faith in the signalman, and although Ernie knew the move to be quite safe, he had still broken the rules. It just depended if anyone else would find out.

All this time though, and despite all that been going on, still there was no sign of movement from the station. Usually Mr Parsons was pretty regular at appearing from his house in his pressed uniform at 7.00am to let the chickens out, after which he would open up the booking office. Across the yard, two men could be seen standing by the coal office. Ernie wondered if they might come over and ask how long the wagon had been there. Alternatively they might ask the Station Master as he was bound to enquire later himself anyway. But for the moment he could ponder a while and partake of his own tea, he felt he had earned it. It was after all the first time he had dealt with a situation of that type on his own and he had learned a lot from it. The errors of the morning would not be repeated. After all, it had been a hurried start.

Chapter 3

THE GUVNOR REMEMBERS

As he waited for the goods to arrive and clear Worthy Down, and then for the passenger train to arrive Ernie was standing up and looking toward the platform. Already he could see there was some activity. Boxes of watercress piled high on a platform barrow and seemingly, from his line of sight at least, almost ready to tip over. Additionally, there were two or three passengers already milling around under the canopy, anticipating the first up train, although it was yet still to be offered to him from Worthy Down.

Unseen by Ernie, but probably working behind the scenes, was Jack Tanner, one of the regular porters whose early turn shift started at 6.30am. Winter times would mean the first task for the early turn man was the lighting of the station lamps, those at Sutton Scotney consisting of oil or Tilley lamps, but this would not be necessary for a few more weeks yet. (On the GWR, these lamps were sometimes known as "Challow" lamps, the name derived from the first station where the type of lamp had been used.) The fact that Jack was not on the platform probably meant that he was already in the booking office, meaning the Station Master had decided to avoid the morning hour.

"It's alright for him," thought Ernie, "he can choose his hours when he fancies a lie-in."

Ernie remembered the time he had spent on the platform as a porter before being given the go-ahead to start learning the box. But even after he had been accepted for training as a signalman, Mr Parsons had attempted to persuade him out of it.

"You work here and get the exams (meaning those on Station Accountancy) and one day you could be in charge of your own station."

Ernie though had his mind made up, and whilst what the Guvnor had said was actually true, it also depended somewhat on whether your face fitted and, just as important, on being prepared to move around as well. This he decided he did not want. He had seen enough upheaval as a soldier a few years earlier and now he was glad to return to his home village, where he intended to stay and bring up his family.

Almost as an intrusion into his thoughts, that moment the bell rang from Worthy Down, "two-pause-one", meaning the goods had at last arrived there. This Ernie acknowledged, and this was followed immediately by "three-pause-one" (even though it did sound like four continuous beats) which was to describe the 7.05am passenger service from Winchester that would run through to Reading via Newbury.

Instinctively, Ernie looked at the clock – 7.22am. The train was then already a few minutes down as it should have been "On Line" to him at 7.18am from Worthy Down, and the request now depended very much on whether Worthy Down had the passenger waiting, or if it was still only just off Kings Worthy. Having accepted it though and completed the booking, a quick phone call to Worthy Down, from where there was no reply, was enough to established that the man there, Ron Fisher, was no doubt out of the box, exchanging the token.

Opposite page – Before and after

Top: Just north of the station, the railway passed over the main A30 roadway by a narrow bridge that, even in the 1930s, was considered a bottleneck. To alleviate the delays, a new bridge was provided at the expense of the County Council and installed some time between the spring of 1937 and the spring of 1938. This view, taken from the north east side, depicts the old structure. The train, possibly the single direct Southampton to Paddington daily service, has passed through the station and is heading north. *(R.F. Roberts)*

Bottom: The new bridge, with provision for an eventual dual-carriageway, although this has never been provided. Today the bridge abutments still remain, although the girders were removed for scrap some years after closure of the line.

(R.A. Collection)

Signalman Jim Hughes in the original signalbox at Sutton Scotney in 1940. This was Jim's first posting as a signalman, and in later years he went on to operate the busy Scours Lane Junction near Reading. The missing location nameplate and the white edge to the structure are both indicative of wartime restrictions.

(Jim Hughes)

This was confirmed just a couple of minutes later by "Train On Line". It was 7.26am and, allowing then for the official six minutes running time from Worthy Down to Sutton Scotney, the service was likely to be eight to ten minutes late leaving him as well.

"Might as well hurry him up if I can," thought Ernie, and so in turn he "offered on" to Lodge Bridge, which was again quickly accepted.

Next he cleared signals 1, 2 and 3, in the frame, "the road" having previously been set in readiness. As it was, the driver was clearly intent on making up for lost time as, no sooner had Ernie finished pulling No 3, the advanced starter to the Off position, than the first of his track circuits, No 1AT, clicked over to "Track Occupied", which heralded the imminent arrival of the service. The short timescale between receiving "Train On Line" and the actual arrival meant that either Worthy Down had been a bit slow in ringing the bell, or the driver was working the engine (and therefore the fireman) a bit harder than usual.

As the track circuits cleared, Ernie could replace No 1, but there was no hurry yet to wander down ready for the token exchange. There would inevitably be a brief time paused at the platform, especially by the time the watercress had been loaded, and so he stood watching as the nose of the engine appeared under the road bridge, followed by its customary three coaches, and drew to a halt mid-way along the station.

It was then with some surprise that, just a few seconds later, there was a brief whistle which heralded the departure.

"That was quick," he considered, and grabbing the token ready in its carrier for the section on to Lodge Bridge he was quickly across the box, down the stairs and then more slowly making his way across the down line ready for the exchange.

This was something else that had been

Jim's fiancée Molly (later of course Mrs Hughes) on one of the many occasions when she would travel to the station to meet Jim from work. Behind is a glimpse of the original ground frame hut, by then being used for parcels, which would later be replaced by the structure shown on page 28. The floral display is typical, not just of Sutton Scotney, but of numerous stations on the GWR and elsewhere. Indeed, it was stated that a climbing rose on the platform side of the goods shed had been trained to form the letters GWR.

(Jim Hughes)

emphasised to him very early on:

"Never run towards an approaching train, you might slip or trip."

Nothing was said about stepping onto or over the actual rails themselves, although Southern men always stepped over the rails, a habit throughout their system where electrified lines were common in certain areas.

The driver though must have noticed that the token was neither in the carrier ready to be collected nor was Ernie on the ground as he had started to move, and as such probably realised the signalman had been caught napping. Accordingly, he slowed his engine so that both signalman and engine arrived simultaneously at the correct spot. The driver was smiling slightly and called down:

"He's sweating off his hangover – that'll teach him to stay out late."

He pointed back to his fireman who, despite managing to exchange tokens was looking decidedly unhappy about the whole affair.

In similar vein to a few moments earlier, Ernie was also cautious to step back carefully as first the tender and then the carriages passed alongside him, a few passengers watching him as he observed the train as it passed. There were no door handles turned the wrong way, although he did notice one person waving, a friendly wave from Miss Taylor, a regular passenger from Sutton Scotney who always waved as she left to go to work teaching at Newtown School a short distance from Highclere. Satisfied that all was well with the train, Ernie was about to turn on his heel and return to the signalbox when a shout from the Guard of the train attracted his attention, and turning towards the last coach he witnessed a rolled up newspaper thrown from the window to land on the ballast nearby.

"Good man." he thought, raising his arm in acknowledgment.

Some Guards were like that, searching the

Part of the "seven-penny" railway. Porter-signalman Jack Tanner (left) with Mr Parsons alongside the replacement parcels shed, probably shortly before Mr Parsons retired. No prizes for guessing which of the pair is going to be moving the sacks!

(R.J. Parsons)

train for newspapers left by passengers and then passing them out to their colleagues as they passed. The fact it was no doubt from the previous day mattered little, news of the outside world was otherwise slow to arrive at Sutton Scotney and he could now look forward to a quiet time later catching up on current affairs.

Returning to the signalbox, Ernie had observed that the tail lamp was in place on the last vehicle, and so he was able to send "Train Out Of Section" to Worthy Down and "Train On Line" to Lodge Bridge. He then completed the Train Register, by which time also he could replace levers numbers 2 and 3 to On as the service would be well past the advanced starter by now, especially if the driver continued at the rate he was going after he had collected the token. Indeed, if the driver did continue at a faster than usual rate, the passengers could be in for a slightly rough ride at Bullington on the way to Lodge Bridge, where there was what the gangers described as "a bad bit of rail" near the river bridge.

But such things were not now Ernie's concern and instead he made busy by preparing the road ready for the next working, re-setting the crossover at the north end of the station in anticipation of the next down train. Considering the brief pause the up service had made at the station, Ernie looked back toward the platform and. as if to confirm his query, he could see the barrow of watercress still intact – it must then be destined for a location north of Newbury or Didcot rather than being routed via Reading.

At the rate they left him, the Reading service would probably be "right time" when it reached Newbury, especially as it was only five minutes late departing from Sutton Scotney. A lot though still depended on matters out of Ernie's control now. It also had to cross only one other service, the first down passenger, which it should meet at Highclere. Provided this was on time, there would not be a problem. The difficulty was when a northbound train missed its booked path at Enborne Junction, then there could be problems as the main line could be very busy at times. The same thing applied at Shawford Junction with the Southern but that was a foreign line, both locations were of course some distance away from the calm of his own particular area of responsibility.

There was time again now for another

break. Signalbox work on a single line with crossing loops was like that; a few minutes of feverish activity followed by periods of relative calm. Time then to settle back for a few moments and look at yesterday's *Daily Sketch*. "Train Out Of Section" was received from Lodge Bridge just three minutes later at 7.34am, after which 45 minutes passed quickly with Ernie engrossed in the news of the period.

The first three weeks of October 1947 had seen the newspapers reporting on items as diverse as the film star Rita Hayworth filing for divorce from Orson Wells, the new Austin A40 that had been introduced and intended to replace the existing 8 and 10 models, and, more relevant to the local area. the Government reducing the bacon ration to just one ounce per week. Unknown of course at this time, but later in the month would come two topics that would be discussed by railwaymen everywhere, regardless of company loyalty; the train crashes at Croydon and Berwick-upon-Tweed, but that of course was in the future.

At 8.23am precisely, the first down train (the 7.45am Newbury to Southampton passenger) was offered to him from Lodge Bridge. Clearly this was running to time and so indicated that the previous up service had indeed managed to regain its schedule further north. Ernie allowed a token to be released for the section leading to him and then made the necessary entries. He would not yet take any further action as the down train was due to cross the 7.32am Southampton to Didcot passenger at his station and he would next anticipate receiving "Call Attention" from Worthy Down. The time to pull off the down home signal, No 25, would be when "Train On Line" was received for the down passenger from Lodge Bridge, and that would not be for two to three minutes yet. Time then to return again to the newspaper.

As he sat in the arm chair, without warning Ernie heard the sound of the door downstairs opening. Every signalbox seemed to possess an arm chair of sorts. Not official equipment like the lockers, desk and signalling equipment of course, but more a creature comfort provided by one of the signalmen and used by all who worked there. That at Sutton Scotney was no doubt typical, once new and the product of someone's hard-earned wages,

its origins were now unknown and it was faded and tattered, as well as having various stains and burns, the result of food and drink spills as well as cigarette burns. The chair was also somewhat rickety – a leg tended to collapse if was dragged rather than lifted to a new position, and indeed, it had previously been located in the original signalbox that had worked the station before 1942. The question of how many generations of signalman had taken advantage of its slumbering qualities was not something often considered by men on the day shifts.

The sound startled Ernie slightly, after all he had been expecting the gong from Lodge Bridge or the bell from Worthy Down, the sound of the opening door was an intrusion into his mindset. Immediately he started to stand up and at the same time put down the newspaper and as he did so, footsteps on the stairs followed by the unmistakable profile of Mr Parsons appeared.

"Mornin' Guv'nor," commented Ernie.

Mr Parsons responded, adding a perhaps slightly cryptic comment about catching him out with the newspaper. Ernie though ignored what was perhaps not intended as sarcasm but at the same time made a mental note for the future. At that precise moment also both gong and bell rang out, giving Ernie the opportunity to deal with the approaching trains and for a moment to avoid any further comment.

Acknowledgments on both token instruments, release a token, pull the various levers, and complete the book (Train Register). Time wise it took little more than a minute or so for all the actions, Mr Parsons was astute enough to avoid the areas where Ernie was either walking to work the token instruments or pull the levers, the fact that trains were approaching from each direction meaning Ernie would need to work alternately at opposite ends of the lever frame.

With the tasks completed for the moment, both men engaged in conversation again, the Station Master enquiring about the noise earlier that morning, which was explained by Ernie including his actions in depositing the coal wagon. The explanation was not fully concluded though, as by now the down passenger service had arrived and Ernie had to attend to collecting the token before checking

The aftermath of the big freeze of 1927 mentioned in Chapter 4. The blizzard (recounted as the worst Hampshire had suffered since 1881) began on Boxing Day 1927 and lasted through until 1ˢᵗ January 1928. This was followed by an equally rapid thaw which caused extensive flooding in other areas.

In the top view, the men are clearing a path within, it was said, the station yard. It will be noted that the blizzard conditions may well have been extremely localised as on the horizon the ground appears hardly affected. In the lower view, the scene between the platforms is depicted, the stacked snow meaning that at the time the up line would have been used for all trains.

this and replacing it in the machine. Next he restored the down home signal to On and offered on the up train before resetting the road once more and then again recording the times. He then repeated the process with the up train at the same time receiving the "tip" from the Guard that all was well and the service had arrived complete. Levers then had to be pulled and the hand generator operated, whilst before departure, each driver also had to receive the correct token ready for the next section, which also involved a walk down the platform insofar as the down train was concerned.

Eventually though he could return to the signalbox, again send the appropriate bell codes on the instruments and, once the trains had passed beyond his control, restore the signals, reset the points (using the hand generator for those at the south end) and generally make ready for the next service, although there was now intended to be a lull of an hour and a

quarter before the next passenger working, which would arrive at 9.51am as the 9.05am departure from Newbury.

Both men resumed their conversation, the Station Master by now occupying the arm chair and leaving Ernie to adopt the typical signalman's pose of one elbow resting on the block shelf. Despite having only taken on that day, his tutoring had meant that he had not only learnt the official workings to good effect but also the general behavioural characteristics of a signalman, including the most comfortable rest positions!

Mr Parsons, evidently satisfied with the explanation over the coal wagon (there was never praise but there would certainly be criticism if he disagreed) looked for a moment as if he were about to depart but instead paused and said:

"Tell me, why is it necessary for a signalman to check the token he receives?"

Ernie was used to this type of action by the man in charge. Indeed he had been warned that Mr Parsons often preceded a story of his own with a question, as if to not only ensure that the men under his charge were fully versed in the necessary operational rules but also so that he could lead in and recount a situation that he had experienced involving the same circumstances. Ernie was quick to reply:

"To make sure the token has not been carried through in error."

"Good." was the response.

Ernie waited, he was not wrong either.

"It has happened twice here that I know of, once years ago with the old box when the instruments were on the platform, and then more recently when they forgot to change at Lodge Bridge and arrived here with the Whitchurch – Lodge Bridge token. Apart from not being able to replace it in the machine here, it might mean that a train could be heading in the opposite direction at the same time. Don't ever make that mistake will you?"

Ernie confirmed that he would not, and Mr Parsons did not elaborate further.

There was then a pause of a few seconds before Mr Parsons asked his next question.

"How about why you should observe a train as it passes?"

"To ensure there are no signs of difficulty with the train or alarms being raised by crew or passengers." said Ernie.

"Absolutely right," came the reply, "and have you ever had the need to act on something like that which you have seen?" he asked.

"There was a door handle not turned properly on an up passenger when I was learning and we stopped it at the advanced starter but no one had fallen out." responded Ernie. "Ron Fisher also told me what to look out for with hot boxes on wagons but everything has been alright so far."

For a moment he wondered if this might have been a trick by the Guvnor, perhaps he had missed something, after all he could only see one side of a train, but Mr Parsons cut his thoughts short by interjecting:

"Good, lets hope its stays that way. Did you hear though what used to happen a few years ago with the Barton Stacey trains?"

Ernie's inner tension abated, this was the boss in a more relaxed state, but you still had to be careful as he could change in a moment.

"No," he replied, "I was with the army then."

"Ah, but not at Barton Stacey I'll bet!" said Mr Parsons. "You see, back in 1940 they were running trains from Winchester through here to Barton Stacey where there was a halt built to service the army camp being built there. With the local builders either serving in the army or busy elsewhere the military had to use whatever manpower was available to supplement the engineers, and a right motley collection of workers they were too. Billeted somewhere south of Winchester, goodness knows what it must have been like near to where they were living.

"They ran a train each way, morning and evening, just for the workers. Don't think the Company (meaning the GWR) were very keen either, as the trains had old coaches from the Southern and a Southern engine as well, funny things they were too, great big chimneys they had.

"Anyway, a lot of these men would get on at Winchester and, because it was such a scramble, Mr Arch (the Winchester Station Master), quickly suspected a fair few were not buying tickets. He tried getting his staff to close the gates at Winchester and only allow one through at a time but that didn't work, simply because there were so many of them and it either took too long or they simply pushed their way through. Next they tried collecting tickets on the return but the same thing happened.

"In the end, Mr Arch and as many of his staff as he could manage, he still had to leave some at Winchester of course, would lock the carriage doors as the train left and then get on with the guard and try and walk through checking tickets as they went. I wouldn't have wanted that job either, they were a rough lot I can tell you. Even then the navvies would try and hide each other, climb out of the windows and even ride on the buffers if they could, anything to avoid paying fare. Don't see what they were trying to save, it was only a few pennies anyway."

Ernie gasped, "Did you say climbing out of the windows; how?"

Mr Parsons looked pleased that his reminiscences had achieved the interest he had intended and continued:

"Well that is what I was saying about watching trains, Jim Hughes and I (Jim Hughes had been a signalman at Sutton Scotney at the old signalbox back in 1940) used to see them standing on the running board of those old Southern coaches and everywhere else as well. Trouble is, although the train was going off north towards Whitchurch, there was no signalbox at Lodge Bridge then and so if we had sent 5-bells 'Stop and Examine' the train would have reached its destination at Barton Stacey before anyone could have done anything about it."

Ernie looked surprised, "You mean they stopped mid-section, surely a passenger train can't do that?"

"They could," replied the Station Master, "you do not always get a station and block post combined. Worthy Down for example was only a bock post after 1942, before that they had a platform on the section between here and Kings Worthy, you should know that."

Ernie felt slightly annoyed, he should indeed have known it and, although Mr Parsons was being quiet jovial, he felt he had made a silly mistake.

"What did you do with the Barton Stacey trains then?" he asked, thinking the best thing was to get the Station Master to continue, although he was also quite interested in what had happened locally whilst he had been away.

"Well, we did stop the train sometimes," replied the Guvnor, "but then all that happened was that they tried to get out, obviously objecting to having been locked in. We were concerned that with them hanging on to the outside someone might have been killed as they went under a bridge. It did not take long to realise though that if they were climbing out here then they had probably been doing it all the way from Winchester and we never seemed to hear of any accidents so probably nothing did happen.

"By the time the train had arrived at Barton Stacey they all piled out and it was all over. The engine took the coaches through to Whitchurch and left them there, returning later in the day when it was time for the workers to go home. Funny thing, although some of the porters from Winchester came back looking a bit worse for wear none of the navvies ever

seemed to bear a grudge. That was just the way they behaved, like it or lump it I suppose."

"How did the staff get back to Winchester?" asked Ernie.

"Oh, that was easy," came the reply, "they went back on the Southern engine, that also meant they could only carry a few, I have seen six squeezed on the footplate of a little tankie, he wasn't half moving as well, think the Southern men were having a bit of fun putting the wind up the Winchester lads. There was another special those years past as well, for the staff at the Bank of England paper factory at Overton. They came up from Winchester too."

At that moment the phone rang. Ernie walked the few steps across to the back wall and picked it up:

"Sutton Scotney" he answered.

"Thought you'd be glad to hear the D.I. has just got on the 9.05 from Newbury." came the voice. "Don't know where he is going but pass it on just in case."

The line went dead. Ernie did not recognise the voice but that did not matter. This was the signalman's "bush telegraph" at work, each man warning the next in line to be on his guard in case the D.I. (the Signalling Inspector) got out to make a surprise inspection. Trouble is he could not really pass it on whilst Mr Parsons was present, there was such a thing as pride.

Ernie looked at the clock, just after 9.15am. He still had until 9.51am until the train from Newbury arrived, that is if the D.I. was coming straight to Sutton Scotney anyway.

"He might stop off on the way" he thought, but inwardly he realised Bob Sullivan was probably going to visit him anyway. He had expected that, although usually it was a few weeks after taking on that a new signalman could expect a visit from the Inspector, just to check everything was in order, and that did not just include the "booking" (the Train Register) but also that the box was clean and tidy as well. It didn't matter that the railways were short of staff nor that perhaps the man on the shift before you had left things in a mess, it would be your fault.

It was a strange line of responsibility as well. Ernie was a signalman and as such worked for the Traffic Department. It was also the Station Master who paid him his wages

GWR PERMANENT WAY DEPARTMENT

Motorised gang trolleys that allowed the permanent-way men to maintain greater distances than in the past were in use on the line through Sutton Scotney during Ernie's time in the signal box This was known as the Motor Economic system of maintenance. Before this system was introduced along with the associated occupation keys on the route through Sutton Scotney, the gangs responsible for track maintenance were in charge of shorter distances.

There was a fierce rivalry between the gangs as to who would win the "Best Kept Length" award, which was judged annually in each GWR division. Sutton Scotney, Gang No 119, came under the London Division and were awarded the prize for the year 1931. This is believed to have been the only time a DNS gang won this prize throughout GWR days.

Locally it was suggested that assistance had also been given from outside, as the Newbury based "relaying gang" had also recently undertaken some work in the local area, which then helped to raise the standard. Whatever the circumstances, the men were justly proud. The gang at the time comprised Harry Purver, Henry Bartholomew, Charlie Hawkins, and the then Ganger, Sam Harvey.

" PRIZE LENGTH "

every week and the Station Master who would be expected to keep an eye on the daily running of the signalbox. The D.I. though was the Signalling Inspector, senior to, but in a different chain of command to, the Station Master. Station Masters were two a penny but D.I.s were only based at a few stations and had a much larger area of responsibility.

"Who was that on the phone?" asked Mr Parsons.

Ernie had to think quickly.

"The gang," he replied (meaning the permanent-way gang), "wanting to tell me where they were working later, then they changed their mind. Think I might hop next door to find out."

"Good idea," replied Mr Parsons, "I was going anyway, I'll sign the book before I go."

Ernie watched as the Station Master entered his signature, as he was entitled and expected to do from time to time, in the all important book.

Both men left the signalbox together, Mr Parsons studiously crossing the tracks towards the yard whilst Ernie did as he had mentioned and went to visit the gangers in the hut next door. He knew they were in there from the wisp of smoke from their chimney and, as was often the case at this time, two men were sitting on the wooden benches, tea cups standing on the table. Sutton Scotney was the boundary of responsibility between the Kings Worthy ganger, Charlie Hawkins and Ted Talmage, his opposite number at Whitchurch, both men regularly checking their lengths and arriving at Sutton Scotney in time for tea.

"Thought you'd like to know Bob Sullivan may be on his way." commented Ernie.

"Thanks," replied Charlie, "we'll be off soon anyway, going to do some packing by the up home, you've saved me a trip. Won't need the key as we'll be inside station limits."

Ernie acknowledged the remark and returned to the signalbox. Grand lot of men they were too. Treat them well and they were always ready to help. Bob Sullivan was not their immediate boss, that was their own Permanent-Way Inspector based at Reading, but he could and would still keep a watchful eye on everything to do with the Company, and it was not unknown for him to report back if he witnessed something amiss.

Returning to the empty signalbox, he could now pass on the message of a pending visit to Worthy Down, which was likewise gratefully received. A quick look around the box revealed all to be reasonably tidy but he did still have a quick sweep up and made sure that there were no foot prints on the lino. (The biggest problem in keeping the place tidy were the marks that the former air raid shelter had left on the lino, which, due its weight, meant indentations still remained.) A trick was to polish a small bit of lino and likewise one of the brass release plungers that were located on the edge of the block shelf above their respective levers.) This cleaning would leave the smell of the cleaning substance hanging in the air, a sure sign that the men were keeping an eye on the housework. Locally this was no major problem, as both Ernie and the other signalmen were all keen to work in a pleasant environment.

The next check was to make sure there were no gaps in the booking, and that things like the windows were all unlocked. (In case of emergency it was no good having to fumble about unlocking a window first, so little things like that, and making sure the hand lamps were full of oil even in daylight were the things that might be checked.) Bob Sullivan did not carry out a tour of inspection like a Sergeant Major, he was more subtle, others might say devious. Instead he would look around, his eyes darting from place to place until evidently satisfied, only then would he relax.

The gong from Lodge Bridge sounded, "three-pause-one". This was the clue the 9.05am must be off Whitchurch.

"Poor lad at Lodge Bridge must be terrified." thought Ernie.

In reality, it was unlikely that particular place was due to be visited, to do so would have meant telling the driver to stop, as usually they just paused enough to change tokens. Additionally, the Inspector would be stuck there until another train arrived, which in turn would likewise need to be stopped.

"No, it has to be here," he thought, "I was expecting it anyway" and walking the few strides to the token machine, he banged out "three-pause-one" in response, so allowing Lodge Bridge to release a token ready for the approaching service.

Chapter 4

THE VISIT

With the last vestige of the sound from the gong still reverberating in his ears, Ernie now turned to the lever frame to make sure that No 18 was reversed – it was. He then looked at the levers controlling the motor points and exit from the loop at the south end.

"Damn," he thought, "I can't remember putting those back, I must have done it when the Guvnor was here just now."

So, once again there was the task of using the hand generator in order to move lever No 11, which, at nearly 600 yards from the signalbox, was beyond the limit for conventional mechanical operation.

Whilst he was turning the handle, there was the sound of beeping from the yard and, pausing briefly from his activity, Ernie saw a number of military vehicles pulling up between the goods sidings. His eyes though were still focussed on the indicator of the hand-generator, which for the present stubbornly still showed Normal on the dial.

"Strange," he thought, and continued turning the handle, giving perhaps a little more gusto to his work. But on this occasion, no matter how much he seemed to turn, the indicator refused to budge.

"This would have to happen today, and especially now of all times," he mused.

At the same time he wondered if he could get hold of the Station Master in the hope of saving himself a walk. Mr Parsons was not normally keen on helping out with this type of difficulty, considering it beneath his dignity somewhat, although if told that Bob Sullivan was on the train that might change his mind.

Ernie was about to reach for the phone connecting the signalbox with the booking

Busy times for the signalman and station staff at Sutton Scotney. 22xx No 2252 awaits departure for Whitchurch and Newbury, whilst alongside is a Winchester, or more likely, Eastleigh bound freight. The signalman has probably already retrieved the token from the crew of the passenger train and would then return it to the machine ready to release another token from the auxiliary instrument at the south end of the loop. This in turn would allow the freight to proceed towards Worthy Down. Working at any station on a single line was often like this, five minutes feverish activity followed by an hour of relative calm!

(R. Blencowe)

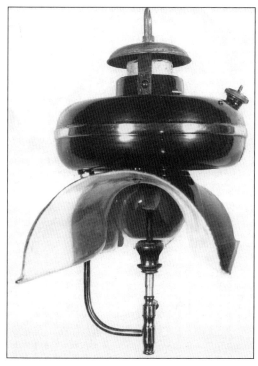

A "Challow" type paraffin lamp, as was provided for a short time at Sutton Scotney; later electric lights were installed.

Operation of these involved pumping the reservoir to pressurise the paraffin it contained – but only at the right moment or else it would pop, smoke and splutter, darkening the glass in the process. Working correctly, they gave a very bright light.

office when he paused and turned on his heel. "Blow it," he voiced out loud, having noticed that the fault, if there was one, was probably of his own making, for looking at the frame the requisite lever for this end of the motor points, No 11, was still standing totally normal in the frame and for the hand-generator to work it would first need to be pulled across to its mid-position.

It was then the work of a few seconds to attempt the same move but this time in the correct order – and of course it worked as well!

A piece of his memory reminded Ernie how he had fallen for the same error as a learner. He could still hear the words of Arthur Watts as well, who had stood back, totally nonchalant, watching his learner do it.

"You won't do that again will you? Well I expect you will, we all have. Bloke who showed me, made me get the handle out and walk all the way down there to turn them by hand."

But Arthur was not that cruel, and a wry smile was all that accompanied what was no doubt a common error amongst any number of learners. Today though there was no one to notice, and it was then but a few moments before all was indeed ready for the approaching passenger service.

Ernie did not have long to wait either, as it seemed but a moment before there were two beats on the gong from Lodge Bridge, followed almost at once by the telephone. Picking up the receiver, a somewhat relieved voice from the boy at Lodge Bridge advised Ernie the train had not stopped and so the D.I. would still be on board. Ernie grunted his thanks, even if inside he was perhaps slightly apprehensive.

Back at the frame, he pulled the home signal No 25 to allow the train to enter the platform and then banged out the initial single beat to Worthy Down in order to start the process of obtaining a token. This action completed, he took the token and carrier and went downstairs and outside to place this in the holder ready to be picked up by the fireman. Like most men, Ernie would sometimes change this essential item by hand and on other occasions use the carrier – a lot depended on if he was busy and equally the weather situation outside. It was no fun standing outside for any longer than was necessary in the face of a westerly gale.

Returning to the signalbox and peering north, he thought he could make out movement approaching, and sure enough a second or so later he had his first sight of what was the

9.05am from Newbury to Southampton slowly approaching around the curve on the far side of the road bridge. For the moment, of course, externally the train was like any other. An engine in dark green livery, its individual number 2240, discernable on the buffer beam even if slightly grubby, followed by three chocolate and cream coaches in a similar dull garb. Bringing up the rear were a pair of what Ernie assumed were horse boxes, although he doubted if they were for him to shunt as in such cases he would invariably have been advised beforehand. (Kings Worthy was the usual recipient destination for horse boxes venturing this far south, where the numerous stables and race horse trainers afforded welcome additional revenue for the railway.)

Ernie watched as the engine and train slowly took the facing crossover into the down platform. He could see the fireman leaning out ready to first of all deposit the token he had brought from Lodge Bridge and then collect that ready for the next section.

It was of course part of Ernie's responsibility to observe the trains as they passed and so, having satisfied himself that the exchange had indeed taken place, he turned his attention to the coaching stock and was able to

Bob Sullivan would approve – clean and tidy. The unfortunate thing though is that this is the interior of Highclere, but on the same line, and with a similar type of lever frame, in that the levers stood vertical, as seen here, when in their "normal" position. No views of the interior of Sutton Scotney signalbox have been discovered and whilst the layout of instruments seen here varied slightly from that presently being discussed, the equipment in use was identical. (Westinghouse)

observe a tall man in dark mackintosh and bow tie standing in the corridor near an open droplight seemingly surveying the scene as the train passed. (Droplights were the opening windows of the doors on coaching stock of the period, and were "dropped" by means of a stout leather strap, the use of which allowed the passenger to reach outside and access the door handle. Great Western, and indeed much other passenger stock of the period, had only a single handle to each door located on the outside.)

As the train slowed to a halt alongside the platform, Ernie could watch for the all important tail lamp on the last vehicle, at the same time acknowledging the wave of the Guard as he confirmed to Ernie that the train was indeed complete and also checked to make sure that no passengers attempted to alight before the train had actually stopped.

Satisfied then that all was well, Ernie could restore the home signal to On and venture outside to collect the token. As he did so, he could see the same Guard in conversation with another man on the platform, although for the moment he busied himself with collecting the token and returning to the signalbox ready to restore this to the Lodge Bridge instrument and then send the "two-pause-one" beats for "Train Out Of Section". The last task was again the noting of the times in the Train Register.

Peering out of the end window again toward the station, there were signs of boxes being unloaded from the Guard's Van, although absent was any sign of passengers. Despite the continued fuel rationing then in place, the trains were not full. Passenger traffic on the Newbury – Winchester branch was often poorly subscribed except on market days and Saturdays when the villagers would travel to either Winchester or sometimes Newbury. Apart from this, there would probably be a few commercial travellers and perhaps one or two regulars, the majority of traffic then coming from parcels such as this morning, as well as freight in and out of the yard. Indeed, the summer harvest of 1946 had witnessed over 40,000 sacks of corn being sent out from the yard in just four months, this additional to the more usual hops, fertilizer, pigeons, bees, pigs, sugar beet, coal and of course watercress, all of which formed the staple traffic.

For the moment, Ernie had seemingly forgotten all about his potential visitor although he was rudely reminded of this when there was the sound of the door opening and a pair of feet stamping on the mat. In effect it could be any number of men although, in reality, Ernie knew full well who it would be and accordingly, with a final quick flick of his eyes across the interior scene, he walked across to the partition guarding the stairs from the operating floor, at the same time exclaiming "Morning".

From below, another voice responded:

"Morning Signalman, alright to come up?"

Ernie knew of course full well who it was, Bob Sullivan, but the D.I. was playing absolutely straight by the rules, asking to enter what was of course an area intended to be kept strictly private. Indeed, to this end, a notice pronouncing this was affixed to the outside of the door. Ernie replied at once:

"Certainly, come on up." and was able to observe Bob Sullivan, still in his railway issue mackintosh, walking slowly up the stairs.

Upon arrival at the operating floor, both men shook hands and exchanged the usual pleasantries and small talk, although Ernie noticed that whilst this was going on Bob's eyes were darting around, not perhaps looking for faults, more like checking there were none. The D.I. could have simply walked in without knocking. There were times, Ernie had heard, when he did – that usually meant trouble. His more usual approach though was to appear and allow himself to be seen by the signalman, so giving the individual time to sort out any last minute matters. Indeed that was probably why he had allowed himself to be viewed at the window of the train and then spent a few minutes in conversation on the platform.

The conversation for the moment over, Bob Sullivan walked across to the back of the box near to the desk and Train Register. This Ernie knew was also his typical behaviour. He was now in a position to read the Train Register when he wished, the signalman had to stand back and operate the box as necessary whilst the D.I. observed from a position totally out of the way. From where he was, the D.I. could not only watch the physical actions of the signalman, but check on the signalman's booking as well.

Aside from watching the boss though, Ernie was also observing the train, which he

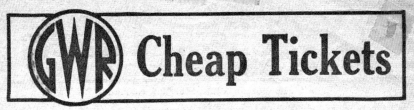

WILL BE ISSUED UNTIL FURTHER NOTICE

BY ANY TRAIN

TO	DAYS UPON WHICH TICKETS ARE ISSUED.	See Note.	RETURN FARES.	
			First Class.	Third Class.

From WINCHESTER.

			s. d.	s. d.
KING'S WORTHY	Weekdays.	—	-/6	-/3½
NEWBURY	,,	—	5/6	3/8
OXFORD	,,	—	11/-	7/4
PADDINGTON	Thursdays and Saturdays.	A	13/5	8/11
PORTSMOUTH and SOUTHSEA	Weekdays.	—	5/11	3/11
READING	,,	—	7/2	4/9
SALISBURY	,,	—	6/3	4/2
SOUTHAMPTON TERMINUS	,,	B	2/9	1/10
SUTTON SCOTNEY	,,	—	1/6	1/-
WHITCHURCH	,,	—	2/9	1/10
WORTHY DOWN PLATFORM	,,	—	1/-	-/7½

From KING'S WORTHY.

NEWBURY	Weekdays.	—	5/2	3/5
PADDINGTON	Wednesdays and Saturdays.	A	13/-	8/8
READING	Weekdays.	—	7/2	4/9
SOUTHAMPTON TERMINUS	,,	—	3/2	2/1
SUTTON SCOTNEY	,,	—	1/1	-/8½
WHITCHURCH	,,	—	2/5	1/7
WINCHESTER	,,	—	-/6	-/3½
WORTHY DOWN PLATFORM	,,	—	-/7	-/4½

From WORTHY DOWN PLATFORM.

KING'S WORTHY	Weekdays.	—	-/7	-/4½
NEWBURY	,,	—	4/9	3/2
PADDINGTON	Wednesdays and Saturdays.	A	12/8	8/5
READING	Weekdays.	—	7/2	4/9
SOUTHAMPTON TERMINUS	,,	—	3/6	2/4
SUTTON SCOTNEY	,,	—	-/9	-/5½
WHITCHURCH	,,	—	2/-	1/4
WINCHESTER	,,	—	1/-	-/7½

From SUTTON SCOTNEY.

KING'S WORTHY	Weekdays.	—	1/1	-/8½
NEWBURY	,,	—	4/-	2/8
PADDINGTON	Thursdays and Saturdays.	A	12/3	8/2
READING	Weekdays.	—	6/9	4/6
SOUTHAMPTON TERMINUS	,,	—	4/-	2/8
WHITCHURCH	,,	—	1/3	-/9½
WINCHESTER	,,	—	1/6	1/-
WORTHY DOWN PLATFORM	,,	—	-/9	-/5½

Passengers return by any train the same day.

A—Will also be issued by any train on Bank Holidays.

B—Passengers from Winchester to Southampton return by any G.W. or Southern Railway train.

For Conditions of Issue, "Bargain Travel on Sundays" and Cheap Tickets from Whitchurch, Litchfield (Hants), Burghclere, Highclere and Woodhay—see other side.

Ernie outside the signalbox, probably sometime in the British Railways era. The nameplate proclaimed SUTTON SCOTNEY SIGNAL BOX and had originally been affixed to the original structure on the platform. By this time it was covered in rust and appears as if it never received a coat of paint in the 20 years or so that it adorned this particular structure.

(Ernie Penny)

could now see was slowly disappearing away from view under the bridge, southwards towards Worthy Down. In a moment it would be out of his view completely, although Ernie could still track its progress from the track circuit indicators, No 25T for the present announcing "Track Occupied", which would later be followed by No 7T and then No 1AT.

With the bars on the repeaters to guide him, Ernie took the duster and, using this to avoid touching the brass bell plunger on the token instrument with his hands, he banged out two beats as "Train On Line" to Worthy Down. Satisfied that the repeaters had now returned to "Track Clear", he took the duster and replaced the starting signal (No 24), and made his way to the Train Register where Bob Sullivan moved aside slightly so that Ernie could complete the record of the departure of the train.

"All done for the moment then?" enquired the D.I..

"For the present yes," replied Ernie, "nothing to do now but wait for the 10.25 off Winchester, I'll reset the road for him in a minute."

Bob Sullivan seemingly just listened and did not pass comment, although a few moments later he added:

"Hear you had a bit of fun this morning, a wagon to come off?"

Ernie knew this was again typical of the

D.I., throw a comment in and let the man give the details. He went on to explain what had happened and how he had dealt with it, the D.I. seemingly nodding in acknowledgement, although Ernie noticed that, at the same time, he was carefully scrutinising the Train Register entries for just a few hours earlier.

With his explanation finished, Ernie stopped and waited for some comment, although all Bob did was prod the book a few times and ask:

"Did you decide to run round the wagon yourself or was this after consultation with the driver?"

"No I told him what I wanted him to do," responded Ernie, "he was not too keen but I didn't let him have the option. They just took so long to get away afterwards."

There was a nod in return, "Be careful though how you make a decision like that in a short space of time. Never rush through a thought or change your mind, that is how accidents happen, especially if you have already accepted the train under Reg 4."

(This regulation meant that the driver would not have been "cautioned" before leaving the previous signalbox.)

Ernie nodded in return, did the D.I. know about how he had changed his mind, or was he just being clever and waiting for a response?

Bob continued, "It is important the man at

Worthy Down is kept informed of what is going on as well – doesn't look like you told him you were shunting into forward section?"

Ernie decided not to possibly dig himself a hole and instead responded about the importance of ensuring the wagon was delivered to the customer and trying his best to get the train away as quickly as possible.

Seemingly satisfied, Bob Sullivan's stance relaxed and, using Ernie's pen, he signed the Train Register as a record of his visit. The conversation became more relaxed, with Bob enquiring how Ernie had settled down, was he enjoying the work and how did he get on with Mr Parsons, the Station Master. Ernie responded accordingly. Bob Sullivan stated:

"Mr Parsons was one of my signalmen here until a few years ago, then he took promotion and I had the devil's own job getting a replacement. Had to use a number of new men short term who I had earmarked for boxes elsewhere."

Ernie nodded. He was somewhat surprised when, almost in the same breath, the D.I. pounced back:

"Make sure you get permission on the block from Worthy Down before you run round – or did you forget to put it in the book?"

It was a bombshell to Ernie, how could he have guessed? But that was why he was the D.I., he was paid to notice that sort of thing, having spent years moving up through the signalling grades, learning all the dodges. Having dropped his bombshell, Bob continued:

"According to the register you did not get permission for the train to proceed south until some time after it had arrived, I expect you told Worthy Down what was going on by phone, but the fact that nothing else was about does not mean you don't work by the rules."

With the boss having established his superior position, and Ernie feeling suitably, chastised, but saying nothing, Bob continued,

"Anyway enough of that, make me a cup of tea and I'll tell you some news."

Tea cup in hand, Bob Sullivan allowed his rank to take precedence over Ernie and sat in the arm chair. Balancing his tea cup on the arm, he reached for his pipe and, after what seemed like an age of filling and tamping, and clouds of smoke that would not have disgraced the morning goods, he turned to Ernie and said:

"Have you ever studied the Train Register here for the months before you took on?"

Ernie confessed that he had not.

"Have a look then for 30th April will you" commented the D.I..

Ernie now turned back the pages until he came upon the requisite item. Scanning the entries, he looked to see if could immediately find what he was supposed to be locating.

"Nothing here," he pondered, "the usual up and down train, release of the occupation key, and a box to box special."

He was interrupted by Bob Sullivan.

"Have a closer look at that 'boxer'," called the D.I..

Ernie did so, his eyes lighting on the fact that it was a diesel car that had passed down to Winchester at 11.41am returning again at 2.35pm the same day.

"The reason I wanted you to notice that," said Bob, "is because the powers that be are thinking again about running diesel cars on this line because of the limited passenger numbers."

"Did they run them before, because I don't remember seeing them?" replied Ernie.

"Well it all started a bit before your time here." Bob answered. "In fact, it was before mine as well, when my predecessor Harry Mealings was the D.I.. The Chief Engineer's department asked to use a diesel railcar for pulling the tunnel inspection van, something about not wanting the fumes of a steam engine in the tunnel at Winchester. Personally I reckon diesel fumes are worse but they could turn the engine off I suppose. Then that gave someone the idea of saving money by replacing the steam trains with a diesel, and so to try it out we have been running one on some of the services between Didcot and Newbury for the past few months. Very successfully I understand as well. It seems now the bosses want to consider extending the use of the diesel to Winchester, so this was a trial to test the timings etc. We were also in correspondence with the Southern about it before the war."

He went on to explain the circumstances that had led up to the April test, which went back to 1939. It appears the GWR were all in favour of using a diesel to save costs, running the whole length between Didcot and Southampton at that time, but as the railcars would be required to work past Winchester and on to Southampton the Southern Railway had to be consulted, and that was the stumbling block.

"We (meaning the GWR) have in our own rule book a note to the effect that the diesel railcars cannot be relied upon the work track circuits and, accordingly, if you were to bring one to a stand, say at your up home signal here, the Guard would either have to use a telephone or come here to carry out Rule 55."

"I still don't see the problem though," said Ernie, "surely the Southern have telephones at their signals?"

"Oh of course," said Bob, "the Southern are a very progressive railway, lots of electrification and the like. Trouble is, their modernisation has meant that south of Shawford Junction the next signalbox is at Allbrook near to Eastleigh, and the lines in-between are all track circuited with intermediate block signals. What they are worried about is that, as we say our railcars cannot be relied upon to operate the track circuits, they could only have one train – our railcar – all the way between Shawford Junction and Allbrook, and that would hold up their services on a very busy section of railway."

Ernie thought for a moment and then added:

"Could we not use them only as far as Winchester then, some of the steam engines still come off there and the Southern takes over?"

Bob Sullivan adjusted himself in the chair slightly and then tapped his pipe out on the stove before he added:

"In theory yes, but that would mean the passengers having to change trains at Winchester, even if we still kept some steam workings as the diesel might not be able to take tail traffic."

(Tail traffic meant another coach, van, or horsebox towed behind.) He continued:

"I was on the test in April and we had one of the Southern engineers with us, we only went as far as Winchester anyway and the object was to see how the railcar performed on various gradients over the branch."

"Was it alright then?" asked Ernie.

"Oh yes no problem there." came the response. "When we got to Winchester I also phoned each of the boxes back up the line to see if their track circuits had worked alright and everyone said it was fine. The Southern man though was not convinced. Apart from the section between Shawford Junction and Allbrook, they also have another set of intermediate signals operated by track circuits south of Eastleigh, and he was also saying there might be clearance problems through one of the platforms at Eastleigh which would be another problem, as well as over some of their fogging machines.

"Trouble is, back in 1939, by the time they managed to convince the Southern that the power and weight of the latest batch of diesels was enough not only for necessary tail traffic but also to operate and treadles and track circuits, the war meant that they not only had to be able to work past Eastleigh but also be approved for any alternative route to Southampton as well."

"But there is no alternative south of Eastleigh." pronounced Ernie.

"Well there is going via Fareham or Romsey even if both of those would involve a reversal," added Bob, "and we had to do that a few times over the years when there was red on. (Red meaning air raid imminent.)

"Then the Southern added an extra complication in that one of services the diesel would work was the 4.55pm from Southampton and that was often made up to four coaches – the diesel could take one perhaps two vehicles behind, but never three. They also wanted to route this service into Platform 1 at Eastleigh, which had been agreed by everyone to be out of bounds to the diesels due to clearance difficulties, so you can see why with so many complications the idea never went through."

"Seems a shame to me, perhaps the Southern didn't want them in the first place." added Ernie.

Bob interrupted "Perhaps they didn't want something modern to be seen in the area either!"

Ernie continued: "But why if it couldn't be done a few years back did they run one again in April?"

Again Bob replied: "Well it was all to do with a new idea and that was to use a three-car diesel set this time and we wanted to try out clearances with what is a slightly different

The oil store at the north end of the up platform. The board crossing used by passengers to access the down platform was also at this end. The goods shed doors had been removed some time prior to 1934 – perhaps they were demolished by a wagon. The yard crane, added after 1906, appears to have been rarely used.

(H.B. Priestley)

design. It was fine, but I doubt if it will be used. The whole thing has come at the wrong time, and Paddington and Waterloo seem to have taken too long to get themselves organised, just not a priority any more. However wait and see, you never know what might happen in the future, and that is why I wanted you to be aware for the future. If they do use diesels you will have to do all your token exchanges by hand as well – just using the key. Put the key in the carrier and there is the risk of breaking a window on the train."

"I'll remember that," responded Ernie, "another cup of tea by the way?"

(In the event, the 30th April 1947 was destined to be the first and last time a diesel railcar ever worked between Newbury and Winchester. North of Newbury the service also quickly reverted to all steam until a few passenger services were worked by diesel between 1960 and 1962.)

Bob Sullivan and Ernie Penny continued their conversations until disturbed at 10.30am as a single beat rang out on the bell from Worthy Down. Glancing at the clock, Ernie realised at once this was the initial call for the release of a token for the 10.25am passenger from Winchester. First though, he had still to reset the road ready for the up line and so, mindful he was being watched, he moved to the frame and pushed and pulled the various levers, together with operating the hand generator so that he was able to finally acknowledge the request from Worthy Down, which culminated in permission for Worthy Down to obtain a

token for the soon-to-be-approaching train. The final act was the recording of the information in the book, after which Bob got up from chair and announced,

"OK Ernie I'll be off then, by this one. It'll be a few minutes before he gets here but I'll have a chat with Mr Parsons before I go."

Pausing briefly and turning round slightly with a wry smile on his face as he made his way down the stairs he added:

"Don't forget to tell them I'm on my way will you?" and with that he was down the stairs and out of the door before Ernie could think of a suitable riposte.

Ernie thought for a moment:

"Now I know why he is an Inspector; knows all the tricks. I'd better tell the others."

Accordingly he banged out "one-pause-two" to Lodge Bridge, ready to impart the information to watch out for anyone alighting from the Newbury passenger, which in turn would be passed on to Whitchurch, Litchfield, Burghclere and so on. Ernie never did hear if Bob Sullivan had made any more calls that day, and so he may well have gone straight back to his office at Newbury.

What he did hear was that, some time later, he had made a surprise visit to Lodge Bridge and immediately relieved the particular boy on duty as the Police were about to arrest him for stealing items of clothing from a washing line. That meant that the D.I. was working the box until he could arrange for a relief man. The boy in question never returned as a signalman.

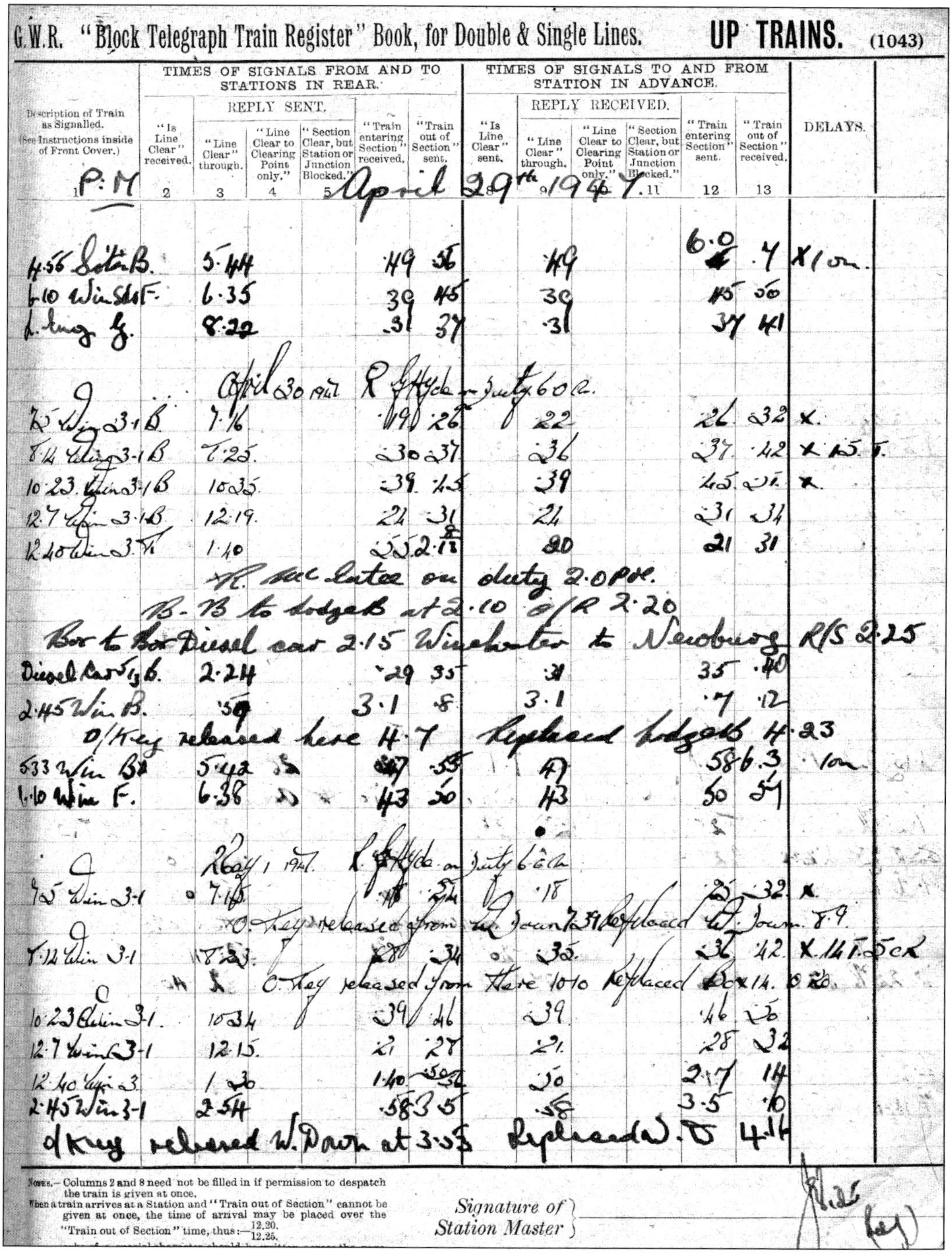

G.W.R. "Block Telegraph Train Register" Book, for Double & Single Lines.									**UP TRAINS.**			(1043)
	TIMES OF SIGNALS FROM AND TO STATIONS IN REAR.					TIMES OF SIGNALS TO AND FROM STATION IN ADVANCE.						
Description of Train as Signalled. (See Instructions inside of Front Cover.)	REPLY SENT.			"Train entering Section" received.	"Train out of Section" sent.	REPLY RECEIVED.			"Train entering Section" sent.	"Train out of Section" received.	DELAYS.	
	"Is Line Clear" received.	"Line Clear" through.	"Line Clear to Clearing Point only."	"Section Clear, but Station or Junction Blocked."			"Is Line Clear" sent.	"Line Clear" through.	"Line Clear to Clearing Point only."	"Section Clear, but Station or Junction Blocked."		
P.M	2	3	4	5			8				12	13

(Date across top: April 29th 1947; columns 11 headed "11")

Handwritten entries — partially legible:

4.56 Soth B.	5.44		49	56	49		6.2	4	X1 on.
6.10 Win.Sh F.	6.35		30	45	30		45	56	
...ing ..y.	8.22		31	37	31		37	41	

April 30 1947 R G Hyde on duty 6.0 a.

7.0 Win 3.1 B	7.16		90 26	22		26	32	X.	
8.14 Win 3.1 B	7.25		30 37	36		37	42	X 45 J.	
10.23 Win 3.1 B	10.35		39 45	39		45	51	X.	
12.7 Win 3.1 B	12.19		24 31	24		31	34		
12.40 Win 3.1	1.10		2.13	80		21	31		

R ...c later on duty 2.0 p.m.
B. B. to dodge B at 2.10 O/R 2.20
Bor to Bor Diesel car 2.15 Winchester to Newbury R/S 2.25

Diesel Car 5.1.6.	2.24		29 35	31		35	40		
2.45 Win B.	59		3.1 8	3.1		7	12		

O/Key released here 4.7 Replaced dodge b 4.23

5.33 Win B.	5.42		47 55	47		58 6.3	1 on		
6.10 Win F.	6.38		43 50	43		50	57		

May 1 1947 R G Hyde on duty 6.0 a.

7.0 Win 3.1	7.15			18			32	X	

O/Key released from ... Down 3.59 Replaced W Down 8.9

7.14 Win 3.1	8.23		28 34	35		36	42	X 14 5 cr	

O/Key released from here 10.10 Replaced Box 14.920

10.23 Win 3.1	10.34		39 46	39		46	26		
12.7 Win 3.1	12.15		21 27	21		28	32		
12.40 Win 3	1.30		1.40 50	50		2.7	14		
2.45 Win 3.1	2.54		58 3.5	58		3.5	10		

O/Key released W Down at 3.03 Replaced W D 4.14

Notes.— Columns 2 and 8 need not be filled in if permission to despatch the train is given at once.
When a train arrives at a Station and "Train out of Section" cannot be given at once, the time of arrival may be placed over the "Train out of Section" time, thus : 12.20/12.25.

Signature of Station Master

The entry for up trains on 30th April 1947, including the special diesel working referred to. The page shown is that for the "up" workings, and depicts the return working of the service from Winchester. In the "down" direction, the diesel had passed through Sutton Scotney at 11.41am that morning. It was signalled in both directions with the code "five-one-three".

Chapter 5

LIFE AT A COUNTRY STATION

Life for Ernie at Sutton Scotney changed only slowly through the years. Following Bob Sullivan's visit, he continued to work either early or late shifts, preferring often the late shift as not only did that give time for attending to his garden at home before going on duty, but after the departure of the 8.01pm to Winchester he would usually be left on his own with little chance of a surprise visit from Mr Parsons. Late shift officially finished at 10.00pm, and although there were no formal booked trains, it was not unusual for a light engine to be advised as a "box-to-box" special from Winchester, which would need to make its way back to Newbury (for Reading) or Didcot. Often these engines had worked a special down to Southampton Docks earlier in the day, sometimes via Basingstoke, and limited line occupancy over the Southern meant it was easier to sent it back through Newbury.

South of Worthy Down there was the connection from the Southern back onto the DNS, avoiding Winchester and Kings Worthy, yet these light engines rarely seemed to use the new route; the Southern seemed keen to get rid of anything not belonging to them as soon as possible, hence they were invariably routed off the Southern further south at Shawford Junction.

Additionally the 6.10pm fast goods from Winchester, which would normally run through all stations as far as Woodhay without stopping, would sometimes need to collect a van or two from Sutton Scotney yard. As it was not booked to cross anything else at Sutton Scotney, this was a simple matter of stopping the train in the up platform and shunting back into the yard to collect any urgent traffic, or even more rarely, deposit any vehicles. Mostly though, such activity of depositing and collecting wagons was left to the daytime pick-up freights, one working in each direction, which, even if there were no wagons to deal with, would invariably stop for the crew to drink tea, seemingly never in much of a hurry to proceed. Again, there were exceptions, such as when the engine crew knew there was a fair amount of work to do elsewhere; then they would be in more of a hurry to be able to devote enough time at whichever station yard the major work was needed at.

As autumn 1947 progressed through to winter, the temperature dropped. Fog and ice were the main problems now, and on occasion it was necessary to call on one or even both his two fogmen to place themselves by the distant signals and have a detonator on the track if a train was approaching the station.

Sometimes one man would be all that would be required although he would then have a hard task making his way from one distant signal to the next at opposite ends of the site. This was fine if the service was purely alternate trains, or trains following each other in the same direction. The trouble came when trains were booked to cross, in which case either a man would be needed at each end, or one of the approaching trains would be held up at the preceding station until the man had reached his post. More usually, the driver of the approaching service would be warned before he left Worthy Down or Lodge Bridge that there was no fogman on duty at Sutton Scotney.

The fogmen themselves were members of the permanent-way gang from the area, who worked for years under the redoubtable Charlie Hawkins, who would sometimes be found in the brick permanent-way hut next to the signalbox. Speaking to Ernie years later, he admitted that after all this time he could not recollect their names, but he did admit that theirs was one of the harshest tasks on the railway, being required to wait out at the signal and "fog" every time a train approached the station. This meant that they would place an exploding detonator (or "shot" as it was sometimes known) on the rails to be exploded by the approaching train. They would also show an amber light from their hand lamp to the driver as an indication to the driver that he was approaching the home signal, which, of course, could be at danger. The distant signals at either end of the station had been fixed at danger for decades and so a detonator had to be placed every time a train approached – but not of course for one travelling away.

Eastleigh District Inspector, Fred Capon (left) at Worthy Down on the occasion of the retirement of the signalman. This was one of three similar views taken by a local newspaper reporter sometime in the 1950s, none was ever published and the name of the retiring man was unfortunately also not recorded. The difference in the position of the levers in the frame compared with that on page 41 will be noted.

(E.A. Sollars)

Having said it was a hard existence, with no hut or other shelter provided, at least it was predictable. The fogman also knew the timetable and so unless there was an extra service (a "boxer") running, the man could come back to the signalbox or permanent-way hut to thaw out between trains. The signalman would also assist the men whenever possible. A telephone call advising how the service was running might mean that there would be no need to wait in freezing conditions for a train that might be running late. The trouble was, one train running late could throw the timetable into disarray, meaning there would be insufficient time to return to a warm environment before needing to set out again. This was especially true with the up distant, which was just over a

mile south of the signalbox and so took some time to walk to and from. Sometimes the train crews would assist, for the driver should of course be familiar with the route, regardless of weather conditions, and as such it was not unknown for them to stop briefly to pick up the fogman and carry him through to the station. Strictly unofficial of course, but one way the men from different departments worked together.

Nationalisation in 1948 brought little immediate change to the working practices either, they were still (Great) Western men even if, very slowly, alterations were made to paperwork and external paint liveries. Still though, stores were delivered from Reading as required (the signalbox allocation being cotton

Didcot 2251 class 0-6-0 No 2201 leaving Sutton Scotney on 20th February 1960. To the left of the train and outside the signal cabin can be seen the "thunder-box" whilst in the immediate foreground is the yard headshunt and where the driver of the morning goods had originally wanted to deposit the solitary coal wagon. As would be expected, the yard capacity was also limited, although eight 4-wheel wagons could be accommodated in the headshunt, 15 in the goods shed siding, and a further 18 in the "back-road". It is believed that some inside keyed rail chairs remained in situ in the yard until the very end. (A Molyneaux / Kestrel Collection)

waste, black lead, two large tablets of soap, four dusters, five gallons of paraffin, a burnisher, two floor cloths, one tin of Brasso, two blacking brushes, two black lead polishers, mops and broom heads). Replacement items were ordered once a week, and delivered usually via the guard on the 7.45am down from Newbury in the morning. Occasionally, this service would have the Swindon stores van attached, although later still (after 1950) items were requisitioned from and despatched from Eastleigh.

Signalboxes can be cold and draughty on occasions, due to the necessary spaces between the levers, and likewise the opening underneath where the point rodding and signal wires would emerge. Consequently, during winter months it was not unknown for an old piece of carpet to be laid across the treads in the vicinity of those

levers not needing to be moved. It helped keep the worst of the cold out, but was frowned upon by the S&T department as they would complain pieces of felt and fluff could work their way down into the locking beneath.

The name Jack Tanner has already been mentioned in the first chapter. Jack starting work at the station shortly after Ernie, and like Ernie first set on porters duties. Afterwards Jack too passed out for the signalbox, which meant that he and Ernie would often share the work between them, although in practice Ernie preferred the signalbox and Jack the platform – an arrangement that suited both admirably.

The years 1948 and 1949 passed quietly. Passenger traffic was still limited, and there were even some rumours about closure, although conversely there were opposing rumours about the whole line being doubled as a relief route. Both of these were quickly scotched when either Bob Sullivan or, on occasions Fred Blackall (another S&T Inspector, this time from Reading) came to visit. Folklore has it that the intended doubling was not proceeded with by the Western Region due to the pending transfer of the line south of Newbury to the Southern Region, whilst another story concerning this was that it was abandoned due to one landowner not being prepared to part with the necessary land.

On one of these visits though, sometime at the start of 1950 Bob dropped a bombshell.

"Thought I would come down and say goodbye." he announced.

"You moving on then?" asked Ernie.

"No," came the reply, "you are – but to the Southern Region, everything south of Enborne is being transferred to the Southern from the 5th of March, Eastleigh will look after you from then on."

Ernie had been in the process of resetting a set of points as Bob spoke, and he immediately paused, his mind full of questions. Bob must have realised the impact his words were having as he continued:

"Your work conditions though and wages will remain the same, what you will notice most is the time sheets will go to Eastleigh in the future, as will takings."

The day's takings together with collected tickets, and other paperwork had in the past been put in a leather pouch which was then placed in a safe in the Guard's van. The other stations would do likewise and with the whole then eventually received at Reading via Newbury.

"On top of that we are planning to close Lodge Bridge, so the section will then be from here to Whitchurch."

It took some time for all this information to be fully understood by Ernie, Jack and the rest of the men south of Newbury. Few were overly keen, but probably much of this was due to fear of the unknown and a reluctance to accept change. Mr Parsons was philosophical:

"The railway will still be here, so is the station, the trains, and your jobs."

It was alright for him though, he would be retiring in the next few years, Ernie had another 30 or more years to go before that could happen.

The early part of 1950 passed with visits from the Signalling & Telegraph department making the necessary changes, ready for the abolition of Lodge Bridge. This would affect both the token and the occupation key sections as well, although the train service was unlikely to change much as, certainly as far back as when Ernie had started, there had never been any trains booked to cross at Lodge Bridge itself.

On his last visit, Bob Sullivan had also explained that, some years earlier (in 1946), the Reading Signal Department had drawn up plans for Lodge Bridge to be switched out at times, which would have meant an extra "long-section" token machine at Sutton Scotney, to be used through to Whitchurch when necessary. In the event, the extra work was not considered justified. Ernie and Bob agreed that they were surprised Lodge Bridge had lasted as long as it did.

The S&T lineman were regular visitors to all the signalboxes, as aside from attending to any electrical problem that might occur, they would also have to transfer tokens on occasions between the signalbox and the auxiliary token hut (at Sutton Scotney this was at the south end of the loop) as well as between neighbouring signalboxes. In theory, such transfers should not have been necessary, as there were the same number of workings in each direction. In practice however, out-of-course running and special workings, which travelled one way and not the other, such as a light engine from Winchester for Didcot, would mean there could be more tokens at one end of a section than was otherwise desirable.

As winter slowly gave way to the spring of 1950, the weeks passed, and it seemed no time at all until March arrived, and with it a tall figure waiting for Ernie in the signalbox as he arrived for 2pm to 10pm duty one afternoon. Having signed the book, he was introduced to Fred Capon the Eastleigh District Inspector who was on a tour of inspection visiting the boxes south of Newbury.

"Did the lads tell you I was on the way?" Fred asked.

"No," replied Ernie, "but the other day someone said you had been around, was it at Whitchurch? – but I though they meant another of the engineers to do with Lodge Bridge being

A bright moment in what was a depressive era. 3440 "City of Truro" restored and in regular service on the DNS line between Didcot and Southampton in the period 1957/8. The engine is seen here at 2.45pm will re-appear northbound at 5.51pm.

(Gerry Siviour)

taken out."

Fred went on to confirm he had visited all of the boxes north of Sutton Scotney and knew Winchester Chesil as well. He hoped to see Sutton Scotney, Worthy Down, and Kings Worthy that afternoon.

"Well," thought Ernie, "might as well start off right.", so tea was made, offered and accepted (the recognised signalling terms can be used for more than one meaning as regards what goes on in a signalbox!), and that of course put Fred and Ernie straight for what would be many years of harmonious accord. Indeed, Fred was partly instrumental in securing Ernie a stores job at Eastleigh years later.

Fred Capon's enlarged Eastleigh district meant he was a somewhat infrequent visitor compared to Bob Sullivan. Eventually, following the retirement and moving away of

Mr Parsons, it was Harry Hillier, the Whitchurch Station Master, himself a former signalman, who would act as supervisor when required, often visiting daily.

Fred Parsons though does feature in our story on one more occasion, for as mentioned previously he was almost fanatical when it came to the station garden, and with Ernie suitably green fingered as well, it was not surprising that the two men eventually struck up a mutual respect for each other's talents. This developed so that on one occasion, when the floral display at Sutton Scotney was so grand that it won a prize in the Southern Region category for station gardens, it was Ernie who was selected by Mr Parsons to accompany him to Bournemouth to receive the award. Aside from a certificate (sadly this has not been located) there was a cash gift as well.

The return journey saw the two men

Porter and Guard appear to have little to occupy themselves with in this late 1950s view. The lack of passengers is sadly obvious, buses and private motor cars having had a drastic effect on services. Indeed, a census in 1958 indicated that in total only six passengers joined and four alighted at the station on a single day. All those who joined headed south. Similar returns were gained from the other stations on the line. It was then but a matter of time before the inevitable occurred. (R. Blencowe)

discussing the day's events in the train on the way back, with Ernie recalling the conversation going something along the following lines:

"I think this will go nicely, towards a new bed of hydrangeas alongside the goods shed next year." announced Mr Parsons.

Ernie though was quick to respond, commenting that half of the work culminating in the award was down to him and so said:

"What you do with your half of the money is up to you, but I know what I'm doing with mine and that's not spending it on your blessed garden."

He would never have dreamt of speaking to the boss like that before, but nothing more was said over the matter although Ernie did recall the rest of journey was completed in an atmosphere of strained silence.

The limited supervision that followed in the 1950s gave the men the opportunity to perfect some side-lines as a means of enhancing what was the none too favourable railway pay. Ernie's was that of acting as local barber, the task undertaken either in the signalbox or the adjacent permanent-way hut, his clientele including not only railway staff but most of the working men from the village.

He had also moved his family into the station house vacated by Mr Parsons. Not with any intention of becoming Station Master, locally that role had now gone for ever, but it was larger than where he had lived before and he had a growing family. Additionally, the garden was well kept and he further supplemented both his diet and his income with freshly produced vegetables, being recalled in particular for producing and selling the best pickled onions for miles around. (Ernie also had an allotment elsewhere in the village.)

Occasionally, things would go wrong with the signalling equipment either at Sutton Scotney or elsewhere, which would mean a time of quick thinking and adapting to the needs of the situation. The most common case of this being a failure of the motor points at either Sutton Scotney or at one of the stations on either side. If the failure was local, it was usually possible to operate them by hand from the ground, although the alternative was to clip and padlock as necessary so sending all traffic through the one platform, which was fine unless trains were actually booked to cross. In the latter case a degree of shunting could be required. If the failure was at Worthy Down or Whitchurch, it meant verbally warning the driver of the situation to be encountered before the train departed from Sutton Scotney.

Ernie was also involved in the effects of the derailments at Whitchurch, which took place in 1954 and 1960. One the first occasion, a passenger train had already left him for Whitchurch when No 76017, coming in the other direction failed to stop at the end of the loop at Whitchurch and came to rest part way down the embankment with its train piling up behind and blocking the running line. Fortunately Ken Alexander, the Whitchurch signalman on duty, managed to stop the approaching passenger train before it reached the wreckage, but this resulted in the passenger train having to propel the five miles back to Sutton Scotney, from where an alternative bus service was eventually provided. Following this, the engine of the passenger train ran round and worked part way back to Winchester, making sure not to hold up the breakdown gang which was by then coming up from Eastleigh. One of the members of the Whitchurch permanent-way gang actually saw the train go down the bank at Whitchurch and was in fact closer to and so in a better position to warn the approaching passenger service. Unfortunately, at that precise moment he was occupied in attending to a call of nature at the bottom of the embankment and so felt he could hardly approach the train with trousers at half-mast. His colleagues would tease him mercilessly about that for some time afterwards.

On other occasions, the work of the permanent-way gang or signal engineers would see various points and signals temporarily disconnected, which would result in either pilot working (also resulted to when there was the occasional failure of the token system) or the services of a ground signalman who would liaise with Ernie as well as the engineer in charge on the ground. Rarely though did the service stop. It ran mainly to time – partly it must be said because schedules were easy, and likewise line occupancy hardly excessive. It

was to some extent harder after 1955 when the economy of that year saw Kings Worthy, Litchfield, and Highclere stations loose their passing loops and so some of the sections became longer. Matters eased though for the final years after 1958, although this time due to the curtailment of some of the services. As Ernie and the others knew, it was inevitable that the railway would close, it was just a question of when.

Before this though, life at Sutton Scotney was really little altered from that as had been witnessed by successive generations of railwaymen. Charlie Hawkins or Ted Talmage would phone up to advise Ernie when and where they would be working, and with Ernie's co-operation, the brass occupation key could be withdrawn by the ganger so allowing them to work in perfect safety without the need for a flag-man, content in the knowledge that no train could use the same section of line. The release of the occupation key locked the token instruments, and no driver would ever knowingly take his train onto the single line without the all important authority of the token.

There was the occasional mild panic when either the ganger was late in giving up his occupation, or the key was misplaced, meaning that the section was effectively locked. This usually happened when the key was put in a pocket for safe keeping and then the man with it went off elsewhere – or went home. More than once, a "runner" had to be sent to retrieve the all important item.

In the late 1950s, an average of something like 12 trains daily would pass through the station, supplemented by occasional special workings. These would normally be freight trains down to Eastleigh and, although the sections were now longer, there were still plenty of spare or "Q" paths in the timetable. Despite the air of pervading gloom about the future, one bright moment was the appearance of the newly restored "City of Truro" on a regular passenger turn for a brief time after 1957. However, this only lasted a year, after which the inevitable occurred and Sutton Scotney lost its passenger service to Newbury and Winchester from Monday 7th March 1960. Ironically, even in that last week the booking office was still issuing tickets headed "GWR", because limited demand meant that they were

WINCHESTER, NEWBURY, AND DIDCOT.

Single Line worked by Electric Train Token between Winchester and Woodhay. Crossing Places are Winchester, King's Worthy, Worthy Down, Sutton Scotney, Lodge Bridge, Whitchurch, Litchfield, Burghclere, Highclere and Woodhay.   Double Line between Woodhay and Didcot.   Junction from Southern Railway (Up Line only) at Worthy Down.
Working of Heavy Engines between Newbury and Didcot.—For particulars of authorised classes at restricted speeds, see page 157.

											B	C	B	B	K	B	B	J	B	K	B	B	B	F	C	B
			UP TRAINS.		Ruling Gradient.	*Time Allowances for Freight Trains, see page 2.*						5.25 a.m. West-bury to Oxley Sdgs. Frght MX	7.32 a.m. Read-ing Pass.	7.53 a.m. South-amp-ton Pass.	9.36 a.m. East-leigh South-ampt'n S.R. Pass.	11.36 a.m. South-amp-ton Pass.	1.45 a.m. Tavi-stock to Banbury. MX	1.55 p.m. South-amp-ton Pass.	New-bury R.C. Frght	Pass.	4.55 p.m. South-amp-ton Pass.	7.35 p.m. South-amp-ton Pass.	Frght	5.25 a.m. West-bury to Oxley Sdgs. Frght	6.40 p.m. Lam-bourn to Oxford Pass.
			STATIONS.			Point-to-point Allowances.																			
Mile Post Distance.	Distance from Didcot.					"C."	"D."	Ex-press.	Ord-inary	Allow for Stop.	Allow for Start.	Pass.						SO						SO	
M C	M C					Mins.	Mins.	Mins.	Mins.	Mins.	Mins.	a.m.	a.m.	a.m.	a.m.	a.m.	a.m.	p.m.	p.m.	p.m.	p.m.	p.m.	p.m.	a.m.	p.m.
25 20	44 27	WINCHESTER { arr. ex S.R. dep. to G.W.			—	—	—	—	—	—	1	…	…	7 5	8 8 8 14	8 32	10x13 10 25	12 1 12 7	2 37 2 45	12 40	5x27 5 33	8 13	…	6 10	…
23 24	42 31	King's Worthy …… { arr. dep.	106 R.	—	—	—	6	1	2	…	…	7 10 7 12	8 18 8 21	…	10 30 10 31	12 12 12 13	2 50 2 51	12 48 1 6	5 38 5 39	CS	…	…	…
21 19	40 36	Worthy Down …… { arr. dep.	106 R.	—	—	—	—	—	—	…	…	7 17 7 18	8 26 8 27	…	10 36 10 37	12 18 12 19	2X56 2 57	1 13 1 41	5 44 5 45	CS	…	…	…
18 33	37 40	Sutton Scotney … { arr. dep.	106 R.	—	—	—	14	1	1	…	…	7 24 7 26	8X33 8 36	…	10 43 10 44	12 25 12 26	3 3 3 4	1 53 2 9	5 51 5 53	B	…	CS	…
15 77	35 4	Lodge Bridge Loop { arr. dep.	150 R.	—	—	—	—	—	—	…	CS	CS	…	CS	CS	…	CS	CS	…	CS	…	CS	…
12 57	31 64	Whitchurch …… { arr. dep.	106 R.	—	—	—	14	1	1	…	…	7 36 7 39	8 46 8 47	…	10 54 10 56	12 36 12 38	3 14 3 15	6 3 6 4	CS	…	…	…
9 2	28 9	Litchfield ……… { arr. dep.	106 R.	—	—	—	10	1	1	…	…	7 47 7 49	8 55 8 56	K	11 4 11 5	12 47 12X52	3 23 3 24	3 33	Pass.	6 12 6 13	CS	…	…
6 33	25 40	Burghclere …… { arr. dep.	124 R.	—	—	—	7	1	1	…	…	7 54 7 56	9 1 9 2	…	11 10 11 11	12 57 12 58	3 29 3 30	3 52 4 9	SO	6 18 6 19	CS	…	…
4 38	23 45	Highclere ……… { arr. dep.	129 R.	—	—	—	6	1	1	…	8X 0 8 6	9 6 9 7	Frght	11 15 11 16	1 1 1 3	3 34 3 35	CR	p.m.	6 23 6 28	…	…	…
2 18	21 25	Woodhay ……… { arr. dep.	106 F.	—	—	—	6	1	1	…	8 11 8 14	9 12 9X15	…	11 21 11 23	1 8 1 10	3 39 3 40	4X23 4 44	…	6 28 6 29	7X15 7 28	…	…
0 0	19 7	Enborne Junction …	pass	106 F.	—	—	—	6	—	—	O W CT	…	…	…	…	…	…	…	…	…	…	O W CT	…
—	17 77	NEWBURY { arr. dep.	199 F.	—	—	—	3	1	¶	6 45	6 41 6*58	8 21 8 30	9 22 9 35	11 35	1 18 1 58	2*5 2 9	3 47 4 25	4 55 5 10	5 26	6 38 7 25	8 10	7 40 8 25	6 40 6 50	7 36 8 10
0 0	17 49	Newbury East Jct. …	pass	513 R.	—	—	—	—	—	—	…	…	…	12 30	…	Z	…	…	…	…	…	…	…	…
4 13	13 36	Hermitage ……… { arr. dep.	106 R.	—	—	—	13	1	1	6 53 6 55	—	9 43 9 45	12 45 1 30	…	2 6 2 7	…	4 33 4 34	…	5 34 5 35	7 33 7 35	8 18 8 20	…	8 18 8 20
4 69	12 60	Pinewood Halt ……		106 F.	—	—	—	—	—	—	6 58	—	9 48	…	…	2 10	…	4 37	…	5 38	7 38	8 24	…	8 24
7 7	10 42	Hampstead Norris { arr. dep.	106 F.	—	—	—	7	1	1	7 2 7 3	—	9 53 9 56	1 39 1 49	…	2 15 2 16	…	4 42 4 45	…	5 43 5 46	7 43 7 46	8 29 8 33	…	8 29 8 33
9 14	8 35	Compton ……… { arr. dep.	106 R.	15	17	19	6	1	1	7 7 7 12	7 15 7*17	10 0 10 3	1 57 2 40	…	2 20 2 21	2 58 3*15	4 49 4 51	…	5 50 5 52	7 50 7 52	8 37 8 42	8 54	8 37 8 42
10 79	6 50	Churn …………	pass	132 R.	—	—	—	5	1	1	…	…	R	…	R	…	R	R	R	R	7 6	…
12 33	5 16	Ilsley Signals ……			—	—	—	—	—	—	…	…	…	…	…	…	…	…	…	…	…	…
14 54	2 75	Upton and Blewbury { arr. dep.	106 F.	—	—	—	9	1	1	7 21 7 22	—	10 13 10 14	2 55 3 15	…	2 30 2 32	3*30 3 40	5 0	…	6 1 6 3	8 2 8 3	8 51 8 53	Q	8 51 8 53
17 27	— 22	Didcot East Junction	pass	106 F.	—	—	—	—	—	—	…	7 34	…	…	…	…	…	…	…	7 20	…
		DIDCOT { arr.		L.	13	14	17	8	2	—	7 28 RL	—	10 20 10	3 43	2 38	…	5 8	…	6 9 Bay	8 10 Bay	9 0 Bay	9 20 RL	9 0 RL

R—Calls at Churn during the period of daylight only to pick up or set down passengers on previous notice being given at Newbury. Guard to collect tickets of passengers alighting.
Z—Newbury East Junction 2.12 B E 2.21 p.m. ¶—Didcot East Junction arrive 3.25 p.m. *3.38 p.m. ‡—5 minutes allowed for signal checks approaching Enborne Junction and Newbury.

No. 3   *135*

Extract from the Summer 1947 GWR working timetable, which remained basically unaltered until 1950. After that time, Lodge Bridge ceased to appear, whilst in 1955, Kings Worthy, Litchfield and Highclere ceased to be available as crossing places. Finally, in 1958 there was reduction in the passenger services, which led to closure to passengers south of Newbury in 1960, and north of Newbury two years later. Even so, by this time goods workings were on the increase, a feature which would continue until 1964.

Despite what appears to be the wealth of information available on the station and its working, there are still a number of obvious gaps. Why, for example, were printed tickets available for use between Sutton Scotney and Mansfield? It would certainly not have been the practice to print a special batch unless the traffic warranted such a move - but what traffic was this?

Efforts to fill in the gaps have also drawn a blank in recent years, a request for information locally in 2004 revealed not a single response.

Even so, two decades past, there were still people around who recalled, travelled and worked on the line, and for their recollections and memories we can only be grateful.

Sutton Scotney may have been but one minor station on a national system, but it still warrants having its story told. If for no other reason than to typify the life of a country station.

DIDCOT, NEWBURY AND WINCHESTER—continued.

Working of Heavy Engines between Didcot and Newbury.—For particulars of authorised classes at restricted speeds, see page 157.

STATIONS.	Dis-tance from Didcot M.C.	Mile Post Dis-tance. M.C.		Ruling Gra-dient 1 in	"C." Mins.	"D." Mins.	Ex-press. Mins.	Ordin-ary. Mins.	Allow for Stop. Mins.	Allow for Start. Mins.	H 10.0 p.m. Ban-bury to Newt'n Abbot Frght a.m.	F Frght a.m.	B South-amp-ton Pass. a.m.	K S.R. Frght MWF0 a.m.	K Frght a.m.	B South-ampt'n Pass. (Mixed to Win-ches-ter) a.m.	K Frght a.m.
DIDCOT .... dep.	— —	— —		—	—	—	—	—	—	1	12 3	4 15	..	..	..	7 39	8 30
Didcot East Junction ...... pass	22	17 27		—	—	—	—	8	1	1 {	—	—	..	..	..	7 45	8 42
Upton and Blewbury ...... {arr. dep.	2 75	14 54		106 R.	—	—	—				—	—	..	..	..	7 47	9 2
Ilsley Signals .... pass	5 63	11 66		106 R.	—	—	—	9	1	1	—	—	..	..	..	7 54	CR
Churn .... dep.	6 50	10 79			—	—	—				—	—	..	..	..	7 58	9 18
Compton .... {arr. dep.	8 35	9 14		106 R.	13	14	17	5	1	1 {	12 25	4 38	..	..	..	8 0 / 8 4	9 43 / 9 50
Hampstead Norris .... {arr. dep.	10 42	7 7		106 F.	—	—	—	5	1	1	—	—	..	..	..	8 5	10 5
Pinewood Halt .... dep.	12 60	4 69			—	—	—				—	—	..	..	..	8 11	—
Hermitage .... {arr. dep.	13 36	4 13		106 R.	—	—	—	9	1	1 {	MX	—	..	..	..	8 13	10 26
Newbury East Junction .... pass	17 49	0 0		106 F.	—	—	—					5 6	..	..	..	8 17	10 58
NEWBURY .... {arr. dep.	17 77	— —		513 F.	15	17	19	12	2	1 {	1 49	6 0	7 45	..	7 50	8 25 / 9 5	11 12
Enborne Junction .... pass	19 7	0 0		199 R.	—	—	—	3	—			—	7 52	8 3		9 12	
Woodhay .... {arr. dep.	21 25	2 18		106 R.	—	—	—	7	1	1	CS	7 54 / 7 59	8X19 / 8 29		9X16 / 9 21	
Highclere .... {arr. dep.	23 45	4 38		106 R.	—	—	—	7	1	1	CS	8X 3 / 8 7	9 40 / 8X48		9 22 / 9X27	
Burghclere .... {arr. dep.	25 40	6 33		106 R.	—	—	—	6	1	1	CS	8 8 / 8 13	9 40 / 9 49		9 32 / 9 33	
Litchfield .... {arr. dep.	28 9	9 2		106 R.	—	—	—	6	1	1	CS	8 14 / 8 21	9 58 / 10 10		9 40 / 9 41	
Whitchurch .... {arr. dep.	31 64	12 57		106 F.	—	—	—	9	1	1	CS	8 23	10 37			
Lodge Bridge Loop .... {arr. dep.	35 4	15 77		150 F.	—	—	—	—	—	{	CS	CS / 8 33	CS / 10 54		CS / 9 51	
Sutton Scotney ...... {arr. dep.	37 40	18 33		106 F.	—	—	—	13	1	1	CS	8X40 / 8 46	11 14 / 11 23		9 52 / 9 58	
Worthy Down .... {arr. dep.	40 26	21 19		106 F.	—	—	—	—	—		7X 7 / 7 20	8 47	11 33		9 59	
King's Worthy ...... {arr. dep.	42 31	23 24		106 F.	—	—	—	12	1	1	CS	8 51 / 8 52	11 41 / 11 53		10 3 / 10 4	
WINCHESTER {arr. ex G.W. dep. to S.R.	44 27	25 20		106 F.	—	—	—	5	1		7 32	8 55 / 9 8	12 0 / 9 45		10 8 / 10X14	

G.W. engines will work } 10.14 a.m. Winchester to Southampton.
through on these trains } 11.26 a.m. Southampton to Winchester.

DOWN TRAINS. STATIONS.	K Frght RR a.m.	B Eastleigh Pass. a.m.		B South-ampton Pass. p.m.	B Pass. SO p.m.	2.56 p.m. Oxford to South-ampt'n Pass. p.m.		B South-amp-ton Pass. p.m.	B Pass. SO p.m.	C Parcels RR SX p.m.				H 10.0 p.m. (Sats) Banbury to Hack-ney Frght a.m.	B Lam-bourn Pass. p.m.	
															WEEK DAYS. → **SUNDAYS.**	
DIDCOT .... dep.	10 30	10 50	..	12 42	2 0	3 35	..	5 55	7 0	..	10 30	..	..	12 3	3 0	
Didcot East Junction pass	—	—	..	—	—	—		—	—		—				—	
Upton & Blewbury {arr. dep.	—	10 56 / 10 57	..	12 48 / 12 49	2 6 / 2 7	3 41 / 3 42		6 1 / 6 2	7 6 / 7 7		—				3 6 / 3 8	
Ilsley Signals ..... pass	—	K		K	K	K		K	K		—				3 18	
Churn .... {arr. dep.	— / 10 63	11 7 / 11 9	..	12 59 / 1 0	2 17 / 2 18	3 52 / 3 54		6 12 / 6 14	7 17 / 7 19		10 50			12 25	3 21 / 3 25	
Hampstead Norris {arr. dep.	—	11 13 / 11 15	..	1 4 / 1 5	2 24 / 2 25	3 58 / 3 59		6 18 / 6 20	7 23 / 7 24		—				3 27 / 3 33	
Pinewood Halt .... dep.	—	11 21	..	1 11	2 31	4 5		6 27	7 31		—				3 35	
Hermitage ...... {arr. dep.	—	11 23 / 11 25	..	1 13 / 1 14	2 33 / 2 34	4 9 / 4 10		6 30 / 6 32	7 33 / 7 35		11 8				3 37	
Newbury East Jct. arr.	11 21	11 33	..	1 25	2 45	4 18		6 41	7 43		11 10				3 45	
NEWBURY ..... dep.	—	12 25	..	2 0	—	4 25		7 14	—		—			1 50	4 10	
Enborne Junction pass	—	—		—	—	—		—	—		—				—	
Woodhay .... {arr. dep.	—	12 32 / 12 33	..	2 8 / 2 9		4 33 / 4X33		7 21 / 7 22			—				—	
Highclere ...... {arr. dep.	—	12 38 / 12 39	..	2 14 / 2 15		4 38 / 4 39		7 27 / 7 29			—				—	
Burghclere ..... {arr. dep.	—	12 43 / 12 44	..	2 19 / 2 20		4 43 / 4 44		7 33 / 7 34			—				—	
Litchfield ...... {arr. dep.	—	12 49 / 12X50	..	2 25 / 2 26		4 49 / 4 50		7 39 / 7 40			—				—	
Whitchurch ..... {arr. dep.	—	12 57 / 12 58	..	2 33 / 2X35		4 49 / 4 58		7 47 / 7 49			—				—	
Lodge Bridge Loop {arr. dep.	—	CS	..	CS		CS		CS			—				—	
Sutton Scotney .. {arr. dep.	—	1 8	..	2 45 / 2 47		5 8 / 5 11		7 59 / 8 1			—				—	
Worthy Down P'm {arr. dep.	—	1 15 / 1 16	..	2 53 / 2X58		5 17 / 5 24		8 7 / 8 8			—				—	
King's Worthy .. {arr. dep.	—	1 20 / 1 21	..	3 2 / 3 6		5 24 / 5 25		8 12 / 8 13			—				—	
WINCH'ST'R {arr. ex G.W. dep. to S.R.	—	1 25 / 1 27	..	3 7 / 3§22		5X30 / 5 40		8 17 / 8 25			—				—	

K—Calls at Churn to pick up or set down passengers on previous notice being given at Didcot. The 5.55 and 7.0 from Didcot call during the period of daylight only. Guard to collect tickets of passengers alighting.

‡—To arrive Newbury at 1.22 p.m. on Saturdays.

§—Departs 3.25 p.m. on Saturdays, June 21st to September 20th.

G.W. engines will work } 1.27 p.m. Winchester to Eastleigh. 3.22 p.m. Winchester to Southampton.
through on these trains } 2.22 p.m. Eastleigh to Winchester. 4.55 p.m. Southampton to Winchester.

still using tickets from the GWR days. (Some of these were bought by people witnessing the last rites and were then kept as souvenirs, never having been used for travel.)

Ernie though still had a job in the signalbox, and the yard was still busy with goods. The railway lorry would also call twice a week under the zonal system, collecting and delivering goods to be sent by rail, or which had arrived at Sutton Scotney Station. It was a long time since the local firm of Taylor's had acted as carriers at the station.

Through freight traffic was also on the increase, which in itself was a good omen. Harry Hillier from Whitchurch was now in charge of all traffic movements south of Newbury and would remain so until 1964. The freight traffic brought its own problems, records showing a wagon reported as on fire on a down goods train, which then had to be put off in Sutton Scotney yard. On another occasion, this time accurately recorded as 22nd August 1962, two tank cars of a northbound oil train were derailed at the station and had to be attended to by the Eastleigh steam crane.

The most serious incidents though were of course when someone was injured. This is known to have happened at the station on just two occasions. The first was when the engine of another northbound train blew a fire tube at the station, with the result that the fireman was badly burned. He was attended to by a local Red Cross nurse until despatched to hospital. The other occasion was when goods guard Fred Crockett lost a foot under a wagon. Again, local help was administered, this time by Winchester driver Tom Keoghan.

The final complete year of service was 1963, but as is recalled by many, this started as the year of the big freeze. Again the permanent-way gang were hard pressed to keep the railway open, even resorting at times to the unofficial use of a salt solution on the points to prevent freezing. Being corrosive this of course was strictly against the rules, but by the addition of smearing oil on top of the mix the action would usually fool a quick investigation by the permanent-way inspector just in case he came to call. Even so, such drastic action was still not enough, and the large volume of snow allied to limited human resources meant that only the down line could be effectively kept clear for all

trains to use. Two of the gang battled valiantly to maintain the through route although, when it was over, the only praise they got was a rebuke for being on duty for too many hours.

The railway had also been blocked by snow during the freak snowstorms of 1927 when the last northbound passenger service was stuck in a drift overnight north of Sutton Scotney. Included in the passenger complement all those years back were a honeymoon couple who had married in Southampton earlier that day. Some assistance was offered to the stranded passengers by a local land-owner who trekked across to the train with sustenance, and then having carried out his Christian duty – left them on board. They were eventually rescued the next day by three engines from Didcot, the first of which had itself become derailed whilst attempting to pull the train free.

Ironically, a few years later in the 1930s, bridge deflection tests were carried out using just two engines to assess a possible upgrade of the line to allow heavy engines to use the railway. This all came in useful for the volume of traffic that would later be carried during WWII – an estimate of 60,000 trains before and after D-day. However, when carrying out the tests in the 1930s, someone had clearly forgotten the time four engines travelling the line coupled together back in 1927!

The start of 1964 saw Ernie and Jack sharing signalbox duties. Still the yard was busy, and anticipated to be more so soon as it was shortly to become the railhead for Stockbridge after closure of the Andover to Romsey line. (In the event this railhead idea did not materialise.) Some idea of the importance of freight in the area can be gathered from the fact that Sutton Scotney was also the last of the intermediate stations south of Newbury to retain its goods yard in use, although it was by now almost entirely given over to agricultural produce and coal. It was a long time since livestock, particularly cattle, had been handled for the local Norton village shows.

In early August 1964, Ernie made another official trip to Bournemouth to collect a prize for the station. The certificate and financial reward were invariably presented at a suitable venue where, in sight of the press, a few words would also be spoken. When Ernie's turn came, he took his place next to officialdom and was asked the usual question:

"Well, what are you going to do with the money at Sutton Scotney?"

The usual, and expected, answer was similar to "purchasing plants, brightening up the facilities" and such like. Ernie's response though was cold and formal:

"Nothing." he replied, "You are closing us down next week."

A stunned silence followed, which continued as Ernie made his way out of the hall and away from the gathering to return home.

Home for those last few days was again in the signalbox. No more would a group of men gather for meals to be taken in the waiting room (part of which had been partitioned off to provide staff accommodation) and no more would the local cricket club have access to the signalbox for use as a changing room. (Ernie would watch the progress of the local team when he could from the rear window of the signalbox, raising and lowering the up starting signal as applause for a fine performance.)

The last train, an Eastleigh bound freight, passed by Sutton Scotney late on the afternoon of Saturday 8th August after which the signalbox was locked up and Ernie's next turn of duty would be learning at Wallers Ash signalbox on the main Bournemouth line. A final stores train was reported to have run on the Sunday to collect items of station and yard furniture that could potentially be re-used. In practice, little if anything ever saw much further use, the number of closures occurring around that time, allied to the fact that many of the items on the line south of Newbury were of WR and not SR origin meant most would end up either smashed, burned or scrapped.

For the present though, he would continue to live in the station house, where changes were slowly made so that it was, for example, no longer necessary to draw water from the well in the scullery. (This was then pumped into a holding tank on the flat roof but would often overflow as well.)

He was not at the station to witness that, within just a few days of closure, Southern Region men were present to remove the token instruments and hand generators from all the signalboxes, the method used being to cut through any wiring rather than unscrewing this from terminals. The excuse was that these were likely to be urgently needed for the proposed singling of the Salisbury to Exeter line. In the event, of course, this was not the case. Additionally these same engineers took a hacksaw to the main cable run leading up to the various instruments and repeaters on the block shelf. Any potential restoration of services was made all the more difficult.

After witnessing official vandalism, it is small wonder that there was unofficial vandalism as well. True, a caretaker was supposedly employed, but he was based at Worthy Down and had the whole area from Winchester to Whitchurch to look after, it was only if someone was on site permanently – like Harry Hillier at Whitchurch, that the vandals did not have the freedom they desired. Consequently, locally windows were smashed and anything having any interest was either pilfered or destroyed. Curiously, the cast iron signalbox nameplate SUTTON SCOTNEY SIGNALBOX survived, it was probably too heavy to remove. When the demolition contractors finally arrived two years later in the autumn of 1966 what was left was pure scrap, and that was quickly removed to be melted down elsewhere.

Ernie too moved on, both work wise and home wise. The trackbed and station site now being owned by Hampshire County Council, who sold the site to an engineering company who established a yard there for over twenty years. To make way for a new office block, the station house was demolished, Ernie and his family having moved to nearby "Brightlands". Ironically the goods shed remained. Eventually, with no further use required for Ernie's work place, the signalbox was also demolished, and another piece of local railway archaeology was consigned to history.

Today, the railway is no more as are most of the characters mentioned in this narrative. The twenty-first century often seeming to criticise the working practices and ethos of previous years by use of unfair and inappropriate comparisons with the present. Perhaps though the most simple and endearing aspect of all was that once, a few short decades ago, this was what life was like at a country station.

Tempora mutantur nos et mutamur in illis

- Times change and we change with them

Also available in the series *Great Western Aspects*:

No 1:   *Burghclere Signalman*, ISBN 095420350X

No 2:   *Winchester (Great Western) - A Snapshot in Time*, ISBN 0954203518